Recipes from **Grandma's Kitchen**™

Holiday Entertaining

Publications International, Ltd.

Favorite Brand Name Recipes at www.fbnr.com

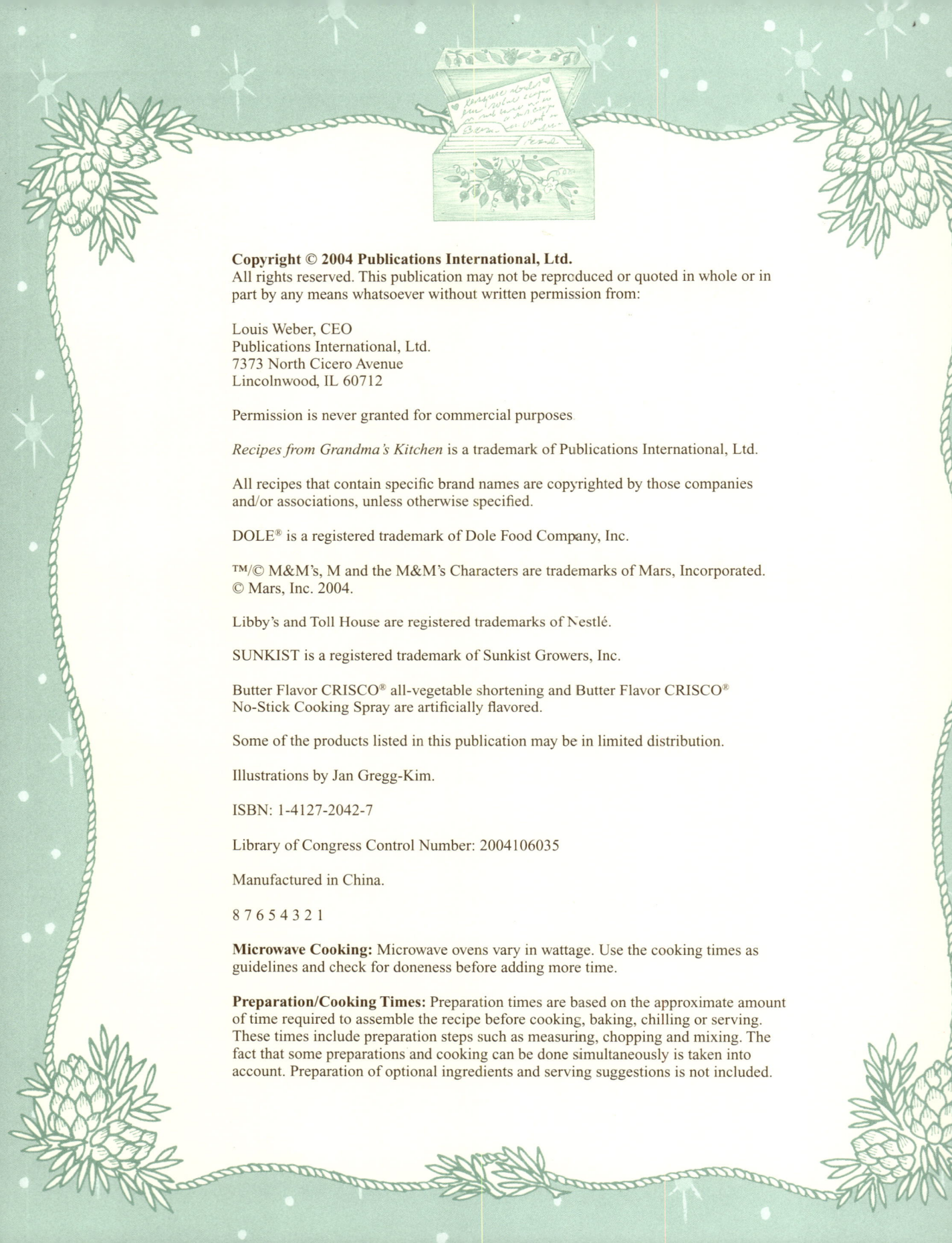

Microwave Cooking: Microwave ovens vary in wattage. Use the cooking times as guidelines and check for doneness before adding more time.

Preparation/Cooking Times: Preparation times are based on the approximate amount of time required to assemble the recipe before cooking, baking, chilling or serving. These times include preparation steps such as measuring, chopping and mixing. The fact that some preparations and cooking can be done simultaneously is taken into account. Preparation of optional ingredients and serving suggestions is not included.

Table of Contents

Joyous Starters

Perfect Roast Beef Wraps

    1 teaspoon LAWRY'S® Perfect Blend Seasoning and Rub for Beef & Pork
    ½ cup light whipped cream cheese
 1½ teaspoons horseradish
    4 large burrito size flour tortillas, warmed to soften
    ½ pound deli sliced roast beef
    1 thinly sliced tomato
    2 leaves romaine lettuce
    2 slices red onion, separated into rings

In a small bowl combine Perfect Blend with cream cheese and horseradish; mix well. Spread two tablespoons of cream cheese mixture on one side of each tortilla. Divide remaining ingredients between the four tortillas. Arrange roast beef, tomato, lettuce, and onion at one end of each tortilla. Starting at that end, roll-up tortilla jellyroll style. Cut into 1½-inch-thick slices.   *Makes 24 appetizers*

Hint: Prepare these wraps ahead of time. Wrap in plastic wrap, refrigerate and slice before serving.

Prep. Time: 10 to 15 minutes

Swiss Cheese, Spinach and Bacon Appetizer Tarts

1 Classic CRISCO® Double Crust (page 165)

Filling
   2 eggs, slightly beaten
   ½ cup sour cream
   ¾ teaspoon mustard
   ¼ teaspoon salt
   ⅛ teaspoon ground nutmeg
   ¼ teaspoon ground red pepper
   ¾ cup shredded Swiss cheese
   3 tablespoons finely chopped onion
   2 tablespoons frozen chopped spinach, squeezed dry
   2 tablespoons crisp cooked bacon, finely chopped
      Ground nutmeg (optional)

Preheat oven to 400°F.

Make Classic CRISCO® Double Crust per recipe directions.

Roll dough to ⅛-inch thickness on a lightly floured surface. Cut with a floured 2¾-inch round cutter. Fit carefully into 1¾-inch muffin cups so dough is not stretched. Press edges against rims.

For filling, blend eggs, sour cream, mustard, salt, nutmeg and red pepper. Stir in cheese, onion, spinach and bacon. Spoon a scant 1 tablespoon filling into each tart shell. Sprinkle with nutmeg, if desired.

Bake for 15 to 20 minutes or until filling is golden brown.   *Makes 2½ dozen*

Holiday Star

Topping
  ¾ cup sour cream
  ½ cup mayonnaise
  2 tablespoons heavy cream
  1 teaspoon balsamic vinegar
  ¼ cup chopped fresh cilantro
  ¼ cup chopped fresh basil
  ¼ cup chopped roasted red peppers, drained and patted dry
  ½ teaspoon garlic powder
  ¼ teaspoon salt
    Black pepper

Star
  2 cans (8 ounces each) refrigerated crescent roll dough

Garnishes
    Red bell pepper, chopped
    Green onion, chopped
    Black olive slices (optional)

1. Preheat oven to 375°F.

2. Combine sour cream, mayonnaise, heavy cream and balsamic vinegar in medium bowl. Stir in cilantro, basil and roasted red peppers. Add garlic powder, salt and black pepper to taste; mix well. Cover; refrigerate 1 hour or until ready to serve.

3. Place 2-inch round cookie cutter or similar size custard cup in center of 14-inch pizza pan; set aside. Remove dough from first can and unroll on cookie sheet. Seal perforations by pressing down slightly with fingers. Cut 24 circles with 1½-inch cookie cutter. Remove excess dough from cut circles; set aside. Repeat with second can.

4. Evenly space five dough circles around the outside edge of the pizza pan. (These will be the star points.) From each star point, make a triangle pattern with rows of slightly overlapping dough circles, working toward the cookie cutter in center of pan. Gather scraps and shape into ball; flatten with hands. Cut more circles as needed to completely fill star.

5. Remove cookie cutter from center of star. Bake 12 to 16 minutes or until star is light golden brown. Cool completely in pan on wire rack about 30 minutes.

6. Spread topping over star. Garnish with red bell pepper, green onion and black olives, if desired. Place decorative candle in center of star. Serve immediately.

Makes about 16 servings

Helpful Hint: For a festive garnish, replace the candle with a hollowed out red or green bell pepper filled with any remaining dip. Place fresh vegetables such as broccoli florets or bell pepper strips around the star.

Pecan Cheese Ball

2 packages (8 ounces each) cream cheese, softened
1 package shredded Cheddar cheese (about 8 ounces)
1 envelope LIPTON® RECIPE SECRETS® Onion Soup Mix
2 tablespoons finely chopped fresh parsley
½ teaspoon garlic powder
½ cup finely chopped pecans, toasted if desired

1. In large bowl, with electric mixer, beat cream cheese until light and fluffy, about 2 minutes. Stir in Cheddar cheese, soup mix, parsley and garlic powder.

2. Wet hands with cold water. Roll cheese mixture into ball. Roll cheese ball in pecans until evenly coated.

3. Refrigerate 1 hour or until set. Serve with crackers.

Makes 1 cheese ball

Prep Time: 15 minutes
Chill Time: 1 hour

Joyous Starters

Merry Crisps

 1 cup all-purpose flour
½ teaspoon baking powder
½ teaspoon paprika
¼ teaspoon salt
⅓ cup plus 1 tablespoon water, divided
 3 tablespoons vegetable oil
 1 egg white
   Toppings: seasoned salt, dried basil leaves or poppy seeds

1. Combine flour, baking powder, paprika and salt in medium bowl. Stir in ⅓ cup water and oil to form smooth dough; refrigerate 10 to 15 minutes.

2. Preheat oven to 400°F. Grease baking sheets.

3. Roll out dough on floured surface to 14×12-inch rectangle. Cut dough using 1- to 1½-inch holiday cookie cutters. Gather and reroll scraps; make additional cut-outs. Place on prepared baking sheets.

4. Combine egg white and remaining 1 tablespoon water; brush on cut-outs. Sprinkle with toppings as desired.

5. Bake 6 to 8 minutes or until edges begin to brown. Remove to wire rack; cool completely.

Makes 7½ dozen crackers

Cheesy Christmas Trees

    ½ cup mayonnaise
    1 tablespoon dry ranch-style salad dressing mix
    1 cup shredded Cheddar cheese
    ¼ cup grated Parmesan cheese
    12 slices firm white bread
    ¼ cup red bell pepper strips
    ¼ cup green bell pepper strips

1. Preheat broiler. Combine mayonnaise and salad dressing mix in medium bowl. Add cheeses; mix well.

2. Cut bread slices with 3½- to 5-inch Christmas-tree-shaped cookie cutter. Spread 1 tablespoon mayonnaise mixture on each tree. Decorate with red and green bell pepper strips. Place on baking sheet.

3. Broil 4 inches from heat 2 to 3 minutes or until hot and bubbly. Serve warm.

Makes about 12 appetizers

Holiday Appetizer Puffs

    1 sheet frozen puff pastry, thawed (½ of 17¼-ounce package)
    2 tablespoons olive or vegetable oil
      Toppings: grated Parmesan cheese, sesame seeds, poppy seeds,
        dried dill weed, dried basil leaves, paprika, drained capers,
        pimiento-stuffed green olive slices

1. Preheat oven to 425°F. Roll pastry on lightly floured surface to 13-inch square. Cut into holiday shapes with cookie cutters (simple-shaped cutters work best). Place on ungreased baking sheets.

2. Brush cut-outs lightly with oil. Decorate with desired toppings.

3. Bake 6 to 8 minutes or until golden. Serve warm or at room temperature.

Makes about 1½ dozen appetizers

Joyous Starters

Honey-Nut Glazed Brie

  8 ounces Brie cheese (wedge or round)
  ¼ cup I CAN'T BELIEVE IT'S NOT BUTTER!® Spread
  1 cup coarsely chopped walnuts
  ¼ teaspoon ground cinnamon (optional)
  ⅛ teaspoon ground nutmeg (optional)
  2 tablespoons honey
  2 large green and/or red apples, cored and thinly sliced

Arrange cheese* on serving platter; set aside.

In 10-inch nonstick skillet, melt I Can't Believe It's Not Butter!® Spread over medium-high heat and stir in walnuts until coated. Stir in cinnamon and nutmeg until blended. Stir in honey and cook, stirring constantly, 2 minutes or until mixture is bubbling. Immediately pour over cheese. Serve hot with apples.

Makes 8 servings

If desired, on microwave-safe plate, arrange cheese and top with cooked nut mixture. Microwave at HIGH (Full Power) 1 minute or until cheese is warm. OR, in 1-quart shallow casserole, arrange cheese and top with cooked nut mixture. Bake at 350° for 10 minutes or until Brie just begins to melt. Serve as above.

Maple-Glazed Meatballs

1½ cups ketchup
  1 cup maple syrup or maple-flavored syrup
  ⅓ cup reduced-sodium soy sauce
  1 tablespoon quick-cooking tapioca
1½ teaspoons ground allspice
  1 teaspoon dry mustard
  2 packages (about 16 ounces each) frozen fully-cooked meatballs
  1 can (20 ounces) pineapple chunks, drained

Slow Cooker Directions

1. Combine ketchup, syrup, soy sauce, tapioca, allspice and mustard in slow cooker.

2. Partially thaw and separate meatballs. Carefully stir meatballs and pineapple chunks into ketchup mixture. Cover; cook on LOW 5 to 6 hours. Stir before serving.

Makes about 48 meatballs

Variation: Serve over hot cooked rice for an entrée.

Prep Time: 10 minutes
Cook Time: 5 to 6 hours

Chicken & Vegetable Roll-Ups

4 ounces reduced-fat cream cheese, softened
2 tablespoons mayonnaise
1 tablespoon Dijon mustard (optional)
¼ teaspoon black pepper
3 (10- to 12-inch) flour tortillas
1 cup finely chopped cooked chicken
¾ cup shredded or finely chopped carrot
¾ cup finely chopped green bell pepper
3 tablespoons chopped green onion

1. Combine cream cheese, mayonnaise, mustard and black pepper in small bowl; stir until well blended.

2. Spread cream cheese mixture evenly onto each tortilla leaving ½-inch border. Divide chicken, carrot, bell pepper and onion evenly over cream cheese leaving 1½-inch border on cream cheese mixture at one end of each tortilla.

3. Roll up each tortilla jelly-roll fashion. Cut each roll into 1½-inch-thick slices.

Makes 5 to 6 appetizer servings

Note: For easier slicing and to allow flavors to blend, wrap rolls in plastic wrap and refrigerate for several hours. Cut into slices.

Crab and Artichoke Stuffed Mushrooms

½ pound Florida blue crab meat
1 (14-ounce) can artichoke hearts, drained and finely chopped
1 cup mayonnaise*
½ cup grated Parmesan cheese
¼ teaspoon lemon pepper seasoning
⅛ teaspoon salt
⅛ teaspoon cayenne pepper
30 large fresh Florida mushrooms

You can substitute mixture of ½ cup mayonnaise and ½ cup plain yogurt.

Remove any pieces of shell or cartilage from crab meat. Combine crab meat, artichoke hearts, mayonnaise, Parmesan cheese and seasonings; mix until well blended. Remove stems from mushrooms and fill the cavity with crab meat mixture. Place in a lightly oiled, shallow baking dish. Bake in a preheated 400°F oven for 10 minutes or until hot and bubbly.   *Makes 30 appetizer servings*

*Favorite recipe from **Florida Department of Agriculture and Consumer Services, Bureau of Seafood and Aquaculture***

Bacon Cheese Spread

½ cup FLEISCHMANN'S® Original Margarine, softened
¼ cup grated Parmesan cheese
¼ cup real bacon bits
¼ cup minced onion

1. Blend margarine, cheese, bacon and onion in small bowl with mixer at medium speed. Cover and store in refrigerator.

2. Serve as a topping for baked potatoes or as a spread for toasted Italian bread.
Makes about 1 cup

Preparation Time: 10 minutes
Total Time: 10 minutes

Toasted Pesto Rounds

¼ cup thinly sliced fresh basil or chopped fresh dill
¼ cup grated Parmesan cheese
3 tablespoons reduced-fat mayonnaise
1 medium clove garlic, minced
12 French bread slices, about ¼ inch thick
1 tablespoon plus 1 teaspoon chopped fresh tomato
1 green onion with top, sliced
Black pepper

1. Preheat broiler.

2. Combine basil, cheese, mayonnaise and garlic in small bowl; mix well.

3. Arrange bread slices in single layer on large nonstick baking sheet or broiler pan. Broil 6 to 8 inches from heat 30 to 45 seconds or until bread slices are lightly toasted.

4. Turn bread slices over; spread evenly with basil mixture. Broil 1 minute or until lightly browned. Top evenly with tomato and green onion. Season to taste with pepper. Transfer to serving plate.

Makes 12 servings

Celebration Cheese Ball

 2 packages (8 ounces each) cream cheese, softened
 ⅓ cup mayonnaise
 ¼ cup grated Parmesan cheese
 2 tablespoons finely chopped carrot
 1 tablespoon finely chopped red onion
1½ teaspoons prepared horseradish
 ¼ teaspoon salt
 ½ cup chopped pecans or walnuts
   Assorted crackers and breadsticks

1. Combine all ingredients except pecans and crackers in medium bowl. Cover and refrigerate until firm.

2. Shape cheese mixture into a ball; roll in pecans. Wrap cheese ball in plastic wrap and refrigerate at least 1 hour. Serve with assorted crackers and breadsticks.

Makes about 2½ cups

Beefy Stuffed Mushrooms

 1 pound lean ground beef
 2 teaspoons prepared horseradish
 1 teaspoon chopped chives
 1 clove garlic, minced
 ¼ teaspoon black pepper
18 large mushrooms
 ⅔ cup dry white wine

1. Preheat oven to 350°F. Thoroughly mix ground beef, horseradish, chives, garlic and pepper in medium bowl.

2. Remove stems from mushrooms; stuff mushroom caps with beef mixture.

3. Place stuffed mushrooms in shallow baking dish; pour wine over mushrooms. Bake 20 minutes or until meat is browned. *Makes 1½ dozen appetizers*

Roasted Red Pepper and Artichoke Torte

2½ cups chopped bagels (about 3 bagels)
2 tablespoons olive oil
2 packages (8 ounces each) cream cheese, softened
1 container (15 ounces) ricotta cheese
1 can (10¾ ounces) condensed cream of celery soup, undiluted
½ cup cholesterol-free egg substitute *or* 2 eggs
2 tablespoons chopped green onion
1 tablespoon dried Italian seasoning
1 clove garlic, minced
1 can (8½ ounces) artichoke hearts, drained and chopped
1 jar (15 ounces) roasted red bell peppers, drained, chopped and divided
1 cup chopped fresh basil, divided

1. Preheat oven to 375°F. Spray 9-inch springform pan with nonstick cooking spray. Combine bagels and oil in medium bowl; mix well. Press bagel mixture into bottom of prepared pan. Bake 15 minutes; cool.

2. Beat cheeses, soup, egg substitute, green onion, Italian seasoning and garlic at medium speed of electric mixer. Spread half of cheese mixture over bagel crust. Top with artichokes and half each of peppers and basil. Spread remaining cheese mixture over basil; top with remaining peppers. Bake 1 hour or until center is set; cool. Refrigerate 6 to 8 hours or overnight. Run knife around edge of torte; remove side of pan. Top with remaining basil. Serve thinly sliced. *Makes 20 servings*

Joyous Starters

Nutty Bacon Cheeseball

 1 package (8 ounces) cream cheese, softened
½ cup milk
 2 cups (8 ounces) shredded sharp Cheddar cheese
 2 cups (8 ounces) shredded Monterey Jack cheese
¼ cup (1 ounce) crumbled blue cheese
¼ cup finely minced green onions (white parts only)
 1 jar (2 ounces) diced pimiento, drained
10 slices bacon, cooked, drained, finely crumbled and divided
¾ cup finely chopped pecans, divided
   Salt and black pepper
¼ cup minced fresh parsley
 1 tablespoon poppy seeds

1. Beat cream cheese and milk in large bowl at low speed of electric mixer until blended. Add remaining cheeses; beat at medium speed until well mixed. Add green onions, pimiento, half of bacon and half of pecans. Beat at medium speed until well mixed. Add salt and pepper to taste. Transfer half of mixture to large piece of plastic wrap. Shape into ball; wrap tightly. Repeat with remaining mixture. Refrigerate at least 2 hours or until chilled.

2. Combine remaining bacon and pecans with parsley and poppy seeds in pie plate or large dinner plate. Remove plastic wrap from each ball; roll each in bacon mixture until well coated. Wrap each ball tightly in plastic wrap and refrigerate until ready to serve, up to 24 hours.   *Makes about 24 servings*

Mini Marinated Beef Skewers

1 beef top round steak (about 1 pound)
2 tablespoons reduced-sodium soy sauce
1 tablespoon dry sherry
1 teaspoon dark sesame oil
2 cloves garlic, minced
18 cherry tomatoes (optional)

1. Cut beef crosswise into ⅛-inch slices. Place in large resealable plastic food storage bag. Combine soy sauce, sherry, oil and garlic in small bowl; pour over steak. Seal bag; turn to coat. Marinate in refrigerator at least 30 minutes or up to 2 hours.

2. Soak 18 (6-inch) wooden skewers in water 20 minutes.

3. Preheat broiler. Drain steak; discard marinade. Weave beef accordion-style onto skewers. Place on rack of broiler pan.

4. Broil 4 to 5 inches from heat 2 minutes. Turn skewers over; broil 2 minutes or until beef is barely pink.

5. Garnish each skewer with 1 cherry tomato, if desired.   *Makes 6 servings*

Hot Pepper Cranberry Jelly Appetizer

½ cup canned whole cranberry sauce
¼ cup apricot fruit spread
1 teaspoon sugar
1 teaspoon cider vinegar
½ teaspoon dried red pepper flakes
½ teaspoon grated fresh ginger
Crackers and cheeses

1. Combine cranberry sauce, fruit spread, sugar, vinegar and pepper flakes in small saucepan. Cook over medium heat until sugar is dissolved; do not boil. Transfer to bowl to cool completely. Stir in ginger.

2. To serve, top crackers with cheese and a dollop of cranberry-apricot mixture.

Makes 16 appetizer servings

Spinach Cheese Bundles

1 container (6½ ounces) garlic-and-herb-flavored spreadable cheese
½ cup chopped fresh spinach
¼ teaspoon black pepper
1 package (17¼ ounces) frozen puff pastry, thawed
Sweet and sour or favorite dipping sauce (optional)

1. Preheat oven to 400°F. Combine cheese, spinach and pepper in small bowl; mix well.

2. Roll out one sheet puff pastry on floured surface into 12-inch square. Cut into 16 (3-inch) squares. Place about 1 teaspoon cheese mixture in center of each square. Brush edges of squares with water. Bring edges together over filling and twist tightly to seal; fan out corners of puff pastry.

3. Place bundles 2 inches apart on ungreased baking sheet. Bake about 13 minutes or until golden brown. Repeat with remaining sheet of puff pastry and cheese mixture. Serve warm with dipping sauce, if desired.

Makes 32 bundles

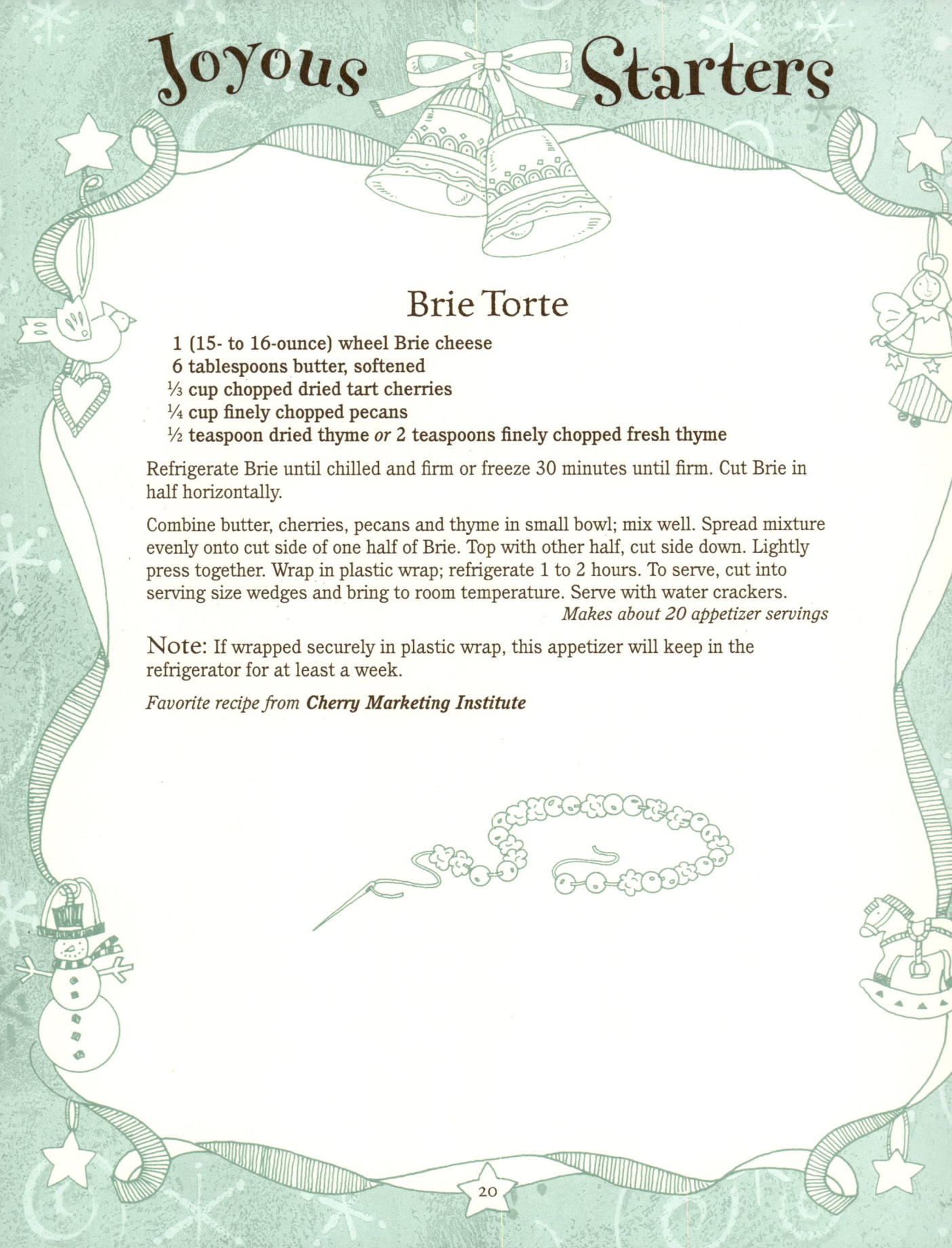

Joyous Starters

Brie Torte

1 (15- to 16-ounce) wheel Brie cheese
6 tablespoons butter, softened
⅓ cup chopped dried tart cherries
¼ cup finely chopped pecans
½ teaspoon dried thyme *or* 2 teaspoons finely chopped fresh thyme

Refrigerate Brie until chilled and firm or freeze 30 minutes until firm. Cut Brie in half horizontally.

Combine butter, cherries, pecans and thyme in small bowl; mix well. Spread mixture evenly onto cut side of one half of Brie. Top with other half, cut side down. Lightly press together. Wrap in plastic wrap; refrigerate 1 to 2 hours. To serve, cut into serving size wedges and bring to room temperature. Serve with water crackers.

Makes about 20 appetizer servings

Note: If wrapped securely in plastic wrap, this appetizer will keep in the refrigerator for at least a week.

*Favorite recipe from **Cherry Marketing Institute***

Joyous Starters

Spinach-Cheese Appetizers

¼ cup olive oil
½ cup chopped onion
2 eggs
16 ounces (1 pound) feta cheese, drained and crumbled
3 packages (10 ounces each) frozen chopped spinach, thawed and squeezed dry
½ cup minced fresh parsley
1 teaspoon dried oregano leaves *or* 2 tablespoons fresh oregano, chopped
Freshly grated nutmeg
Salt and black pepper
1 package (16 ounces) frozen phyllo dough, at room temperature
2 cups margarine, melted

1. Preheat oven to 375°F. Heat oil in small skillet over medium-high heat. Add onion; cook and stir until translucent. Beat eggs in large bowl; stir in onion, feta cheese, spinach, parsley and oregano. Season to taste with nutmeg, salt and pepper.

2. Remove phyllo dough from package; unroll and place on large sheet of waxed paper. Fold phyllo crosswise into thirds. Use scissors to cut along folds into thirds. Cover phyllo with large sheet of plastic wrap and damp clean kitchen towel. Lay 1 strip of phyllo at a time on a flat surface and brush with melted margarine. Fold strip in half lengthwise; brush with margarine again. Place rounded teaspoonful of spinach filling on 1 end of strip; fold over one corner to make triangle. Continue folding end to end, as you would fold a flag, keeping edges straight. Brush top with margarine. Repeat process until all filling is used.

3. Place triangles in single layer seam side down on baking sheet. Bake 20 minutes or until lightly browned. Serve warm.   *Makes 5 dozen appetizers*

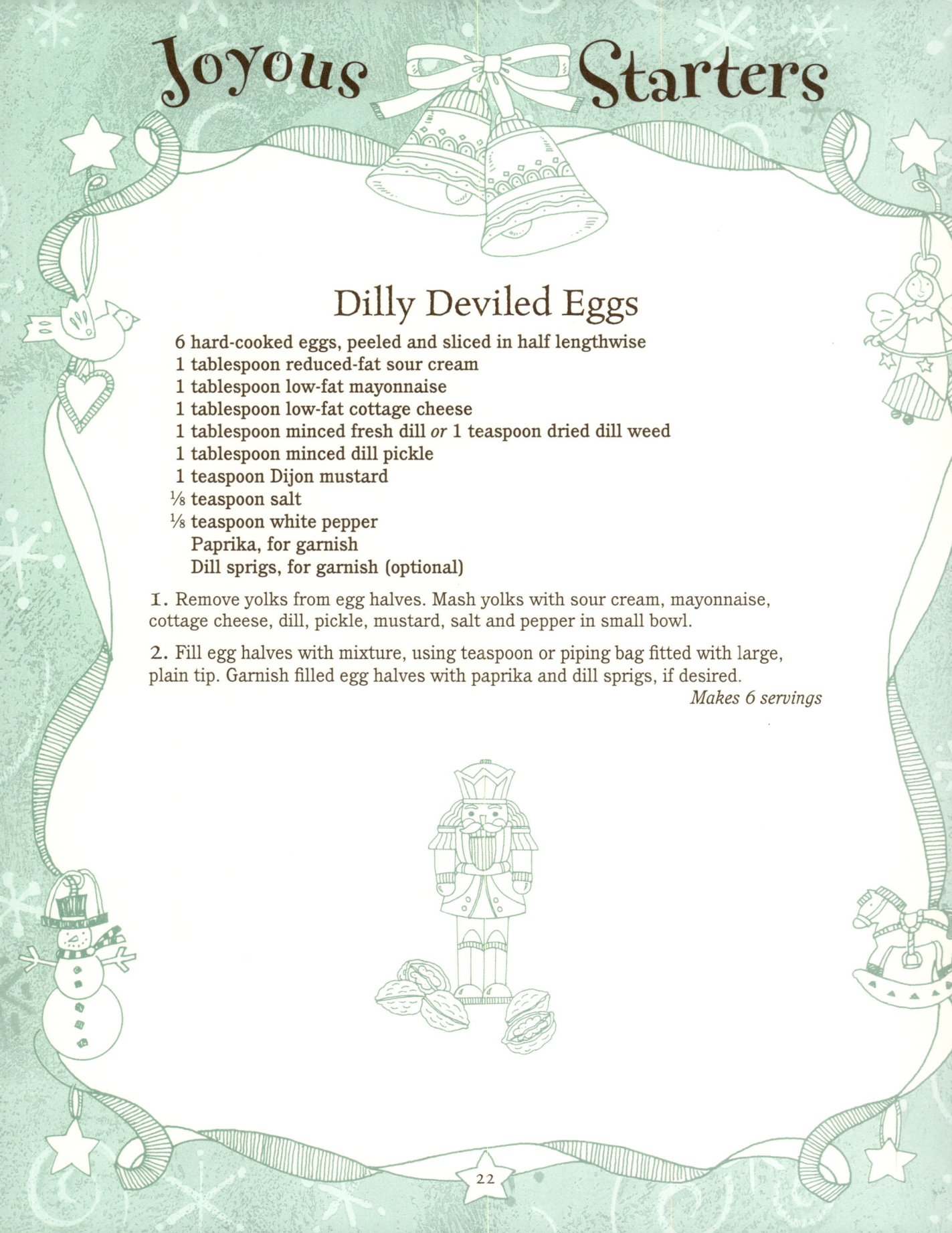

Dilly Deviled Eggs

6 hard-cooked eggs, peeled and sliced in half lengthwise
1 tablespoon reduced-fat sour cream
1 tablespoon low-fat mayonnaise
1 tablespoon low-fat cottage cheese
1 tablespoon minced fresh dill *or* 1 teaspoon dried dill weed
1 tablespoon minced dill pickle
1 teaspoon Dijon mustard
⅛ teaspoon salt
⅛ teaspoon white pepper
   Paprika, for garnish
   Dill sprigs, for garnish (optional)

1. Remove yolks from egg halves. Mash yolks with sour cream, mayonnaise, cottage cheese, dill, pickle, mustard, salt and pepper in small bowl.

2. Fill egg halves with mixture, using teaspoon or piping bag fitted with large, plain tip. Garnish filled egg halves with paprika and dill sprigs, if desired.

Makes 6 servings

Holiday Appetizer Quiche

Crust
  2 cups all-purpose flour
  1 teaspoon salt
  ¾ Butter Flavor CRISCO® Stick or ¾ cup Butter Flavor CRISCO® all-vegetable
     shortening plus additional for greasing
  5 tablespoons cold water

Filling
  2 cups (8 ounces) shredded Swiss cheese
  ⅔ cup chopped ham, crumbled cooked sausage, diced pepperoni
     or crumbled cooked bacon
  ¾ cup thinly sliced green onions (including tops)
  ¼ cup snipped fresh parsley
  1 jar (4 ounces) diced pimientos, well drained
  5 eggs
  1 cup whipping cream
  1 cup half-and-half
  1 teaspoon salt
  ¼ teaspoon pepper

1. Heat oven to 400°F.

2. For crust, combine flour and salt in medium bowl. Cut in ¾ cup shortening using pastry blender (or 2 knives) until all flour is blended in to form pea-size chunks. Sprinkle with water, 1 tablespoon at a time. Toss lightly with fork until dough forms ball.

3. Roll out dough to fit 15×10-inch jelly-roll pan. Place dough in greased pan, folding edges under. Flute edges. Prick crust with fork.

4. For filling, sprinkle cheese, ham, onions, parsley and pimientos evenly over crust. Beat eggs, cream, half-and-half, salt and pepper in medium bowl. Pour over filled crust.

5. Bake at 400°F for 25 to 30 minutes or until set. *Do not overbake.* Cool 5 to 10 minutes. Cut into 2×1½-inch pieces. Serve warm.   *Makes about 50 appetizers*

Note: Crust may bubble during baking and need to be pricked with fork again.

Nutty Stuffed Mushroom Caps

18 large mushrooms (about 1 pound), stems removed and chopped
¼ cup reduced-sodium chicken broth
¼ cup chopped shallots
1 plum tomato or other small tomato, diced
⅓ cup chopped California walnuts
⅔ cup fat-free mayonnaise
1½ cups fresh white bread crumbs
1 tablespoon chopped fresh tarragon *or* 1 teaspoon dried tarragon
Salt and pepper to taste

Preheat oven to 375°F. Coat a large nonstick skillet with nonstick cooking spray. Heat over medium-high heat until hot. Add mushroom caps and cook about 1 minute on each side or until faintly browned. Place mushroom caps on a baking sheet.

Return pan to heat and add broth. When broth is boiling, add stems and shallots and cook 2 to 3 minutes or until most of the liquid has evaporated. Scrape mixture into a bowl and add tomato, walnuts, mayonnaise, bread crumbs and tarragon. Stir to combine; season with salt and pepper.

Mound 1 generous tablespoon of walnut mixture into each mushroom cap. Bake 15 to 18 minutes or until mushrooms are tender. If desired, broil briefly to brown tops lightly. Serve warm or at room temperature.   *Makes 6 servings*

Favorite recipe from **Walnut Marketing Board**

Cheese in a Jar

1 pound (16 ounces) feta cheese, cubed
½ cup extra-virgin olive oil
2 tablespoons finely minced green bell pepper
2 tablespoons finely minced red bell pepper
2 to 3 cloves garlic, finely minced
1 tablespoon Italian flatleaf parsley leaves *or* 1 teaspoon dried parsley
2 teaspoons fresh rosemary *or* 1 teaspoon dried rosemary
1 teaspoon peppercorns
½ teaspoon red pepper flakes
¼ teaspoon salt
¼ teaspoon black pepper

1. Place all ingredients in clean, dry, large glass jar with tight-fitting lid. Marinate in refrigerator several hours or up to several days. Turn jar over occasionally to immerse cheese in seasonings and oil.

2. Serve with toasted baguette slices, crackers, fruit or vegetables, if desired. As cheese is used up, additional cubed cheese can be added to jar, or remaining herb-oil mixture can be made into vinaigrette dressing by adding vinegar to the jar. Shake jar before serving.
Makes 8 servings

Holiday Cheese Tree with Pita Cutouts

1 package (8 ounces) cream cheese, softened
2 cups (8 ounces) shredded Cheddar cheese
3 tablespoons finely chopped red bell pepper
3 tablespoons finely chopped onion
1 tablespoon lemon juice
2 teaspoons Worcestershire sauce
¾ cup chopped fresh parsley
   Red and yellow bell peppers
   Cherry tomatoes, halved
   Pita Cutouts (page 27)

1. Combine cheeses, bell pepper, onion, lemon juice and Worcestershire sauce in medium bowl; mix until well blended. Place on plate. Shape with hands to form cone shape, about 6 inches tall.

2. Press parsley evenly onto cheese tree.

3. Using small ½- to ¾-inch star- and candy-cane-shaped cookie cutters or sharp knife, cut bell peppers into desired shapes. Press shapes and cherry tomatoes onto tree for decorations.

4. Serve with Pita Cutouts.   *Makes about 5 cups (14 to 16 appetizer servings)*

Pita Cutouts

6 pita breads, split in half horizontally
  Olive oil
¼ cup grated Parmesan cheese

1. Preheat oven to 325°F.

2. Using 3-inch cookie cutters or sharp knife, cut pita breads into star, tree and bell shapes. Place in single layer on baking sheet. Lightly brush tops with oil; sprinkle evenly with cheese.

3. Bake 15 to 20 minutes or until crisp. Remove to wire racks; cool completely.

Makes about 4 dozen cut-outs

Note: Use kitchen scissors to easily split pita breads in half.

Marinated Mushrooms

2 pounds mushrooms
1 bottle (8 ounces) Italian salad dressing
  Grated peel of ½ SUNKIST® lemon
  Juice of 1 SUNKIST® lemon
2 tablespoons sliced pimiento (optional)
2 tablespoons chopped parsley

In large saucepan, combine mushrooms and Italian dressing; bring to a boil. Cook, uncovered, 2 to 3 minutes, stirring constantly. Add lemon peel, juice and pimiento. Chill 4 hours or more. Drain; reserve dressing. Stir in parsley. Serve as an appetizer with toothpicks. Garnish with lemon cartwheel slices, if desired.

Makes about 4 cups

Note: Reserved dressing may be used on salads. Makes about 1½ cups.

Variation: Substitute 1 bottle (8 ounces) reduced-calorie Italian dressing for regular Italian dressing.

Roasted Garlic & Spinach Spirals

1 whole head fresh garlic
3 cups fresh spinach leaves
1 can (15 ounces) white beans, rinsed and drained
1 teaspoon dried oregano leaves
¼ teaspoon black pepper
⅛ teaspoon ground red pepper
7 (7-inch) flour tortillas

1. Preheat oven to 400°F. Trim top of garlic just enough to cut tips off center cloves; discard. Moisten head of garlic with water; wrap in foil. Bake 45 minutes or until garlic is soft; cool. Remove garlic from skin by squeezing between fingers and thumb; place in food processor.

2. Rinse spinach leaves; pat dry with paper towels. Remove stems; discard. Finely shred leaves by stacking and cutting several leaves at a time. Place in medium bowl.

3. Add beans, oregano, black pepper and red pepper to food processor; process until smooth. Add to spinach; mix well. Spread mixture evenly onto tortillas; roll up. Trim ½ inch off ends of rolls; discard. Cut rolls into 1-inch pieces. Transfer to serving plates; garnish, if desired. *Makes 10 servings*

Tip: For best results, wrap tortilla rolls in plastic wrap and refrigerate 1 to 2 hours before slicing.

Chicken and Rice Puffs

1 box frozen puff pastry shells, thawed
1 package (about 6 ounces) long grain and wild rice
2 cups cubed cooked chicken
½ (10¾-ounce) can condensed cream of chicken soup, undiluted
⅓ cup chopped slivered almonds, toasted
⅓ cup diced celery
⅓ cup diced red bell pepper
⅓ cup chopped fresh parsley
¼ cup diced onion
¼ cup white wine or chicken broth
2 tablespoons half-and-half (optional)

1. Bake pastry shells according to package directions. Keep warm.

2. Prepare rice according to package directions.

3. Add remaining ingredients to rice; mix well. Cook 4 to 5 minutes until hot and bubbly. Fill pastry shells with rice mixture. Serve immediately.

Makes 6 servings

Tip: This recipe is a great way to use up leftover chicken.

Sausage Roll-Ups

Filling
- ¼ pound ground seasoned sausage, crumbled
- ½ cup chopped mushrooms
- 3 tablespoons chopped onion
- 2 tablespoons finely chopped celery
- 1 tablespoon chopped stuffed green olives
- 2 teaspoons all-purpose flour

Dough
- 1 cup all-purpose flour
- 1 teaspoon baking powder
- 1 teaspoon dried parsley flakes
- ¼ teaspoon salt
- ¼ cup Butter Flavor CRISCO® All-Vegetable Shortening
       or ¼ Butter Flavor CRISCO® Stick, well chilled
- ¼ cup milk

Topping
- 2 tablespoons Butter Flavor CRISCO® Shortening, melted
  Paprika

For filling, in small skillet combine sausage, mushrooms, onion, celery and olives. Cook and stir over medium-high heat until sausage is no longer pink. Stir in flour. Remove from heat. Set aside.

Preheat oven to 350°F. Lightly grease baking sheet. Set aside.

For dough, in medium mixing bowl combine flour, baking powder, parsley flakes and salt. Cut in well-chilled Butter Flavor CRISCO® to form coarse crumbs. Add milk, mixing with fork until particles are moistened and cling together. Form dough* into ball. On floured board, knead 8 to 10 times.

To assemble roll-ups

Roll dough into a 12×16-inch rectangle. Spread filling on dough. Starting with longer side, roll up tightly.**

Cut into ½-inch slices. Place on baking sheet. Brush with melted Butter Flavor CRISCO®. Sprinkle lightly with paprika. Bake at 350°F for 15 to 18 minutes, or until firm. *Make 2½ dozen*

Dough may also be made in a food processor fitted with a metal blade, pulse to mix.

**Can be made a day ahead to this point. Wrap roll tightly in plastic wrap and refrigerate until ready to bake*

Nutty Carrot Spread

¼ cup finely chopped pecans
6 ounces fat-free cream cheese, softened
2 tablespoons frozen orange juice concentrate, thawed
¼ teaspoon ground cinnamon
1 cup shredded carrot
¼ cup raisins
36 party pumpernickel bread slices, toasted, or melba toast rounds

1. Preheat oven to 350°F. Place pecans in shallow baking pan. Bake 10 minutes or until lightly toasted, stirring occasionally.

2. Meanwhile, combine cream cheese, orange juice concentrate and cinnamon in small bowl; stir until well blended. Stir in carrot, pecans and raisins.

3. Spread about 1 tablespoon cream cheese mixture onto each bread slice. Garnish, if desired. *Makes 18 servings*

Splendid Sides

Corn Pudding Soufflé

2 tablespoons butter or margarine
2 tablespoons all-purpose flour
   Half-and-half
1 can (17 ounces) whole kernel corn, drained, liquid reserved
¼ cup canned chopped green chilies, drained
   Dash garlic powder
2 eggs, separated
¼ cup cream-style cottage cheese

I. Preheat oven to 350°F. Melt butter in medium saucepan over medium heat. Stir in flour until smooth. Add enough half-and-half to corn liquid to measure 1 cup. Gradually stir liquid into saucepan. Continue stirring until sauce is smooth and hot. Stir in corn, chilies and garlic powder.

2. Bring corn mixture to a boil over medium heat, stirring constantly. Reduce heat to low. Beat egg yolks in small bowl. Stir about ¼ cup of hot sauce into egg yolks, beating constantly. Stir egg yolk mixture back into sauce. Remove from heat; stir in cottage cheese. Beat egg whites in narrow bowl until stiff peaks form. Fold egg whites into corn mixture. Pour into *ungreased* 1½-quart soufflé dish. Bake 30 minutes or until toothpick inserted in center comes out clean.

Makes 4 to 6 servings

Sweet Potatoes with Cranberry-Ginger Glaze

    2 medium sweet potatoes
    ½ cup dried cranberries
    ¼ cup cranberry juice
    ¼ cup maple syrup
    2 slices (⅛ inch thick) fresh ginger
      Dash black pepper

1. Pierce potatoes all over with fork. Microwave at HIGH 10 minutes or until soft. Peel and cut potatoes into eighths; place in serving dish.

2. Meanwhile, prepare glaze. Place cranberries, juice, syrup, ginger and pepper in small saucepan. Cook over low heat 7 to 10 minutes or until liquid is syrupy. Discard ginger slices. Pour glaze over potatoes. *Makes 4 servings*

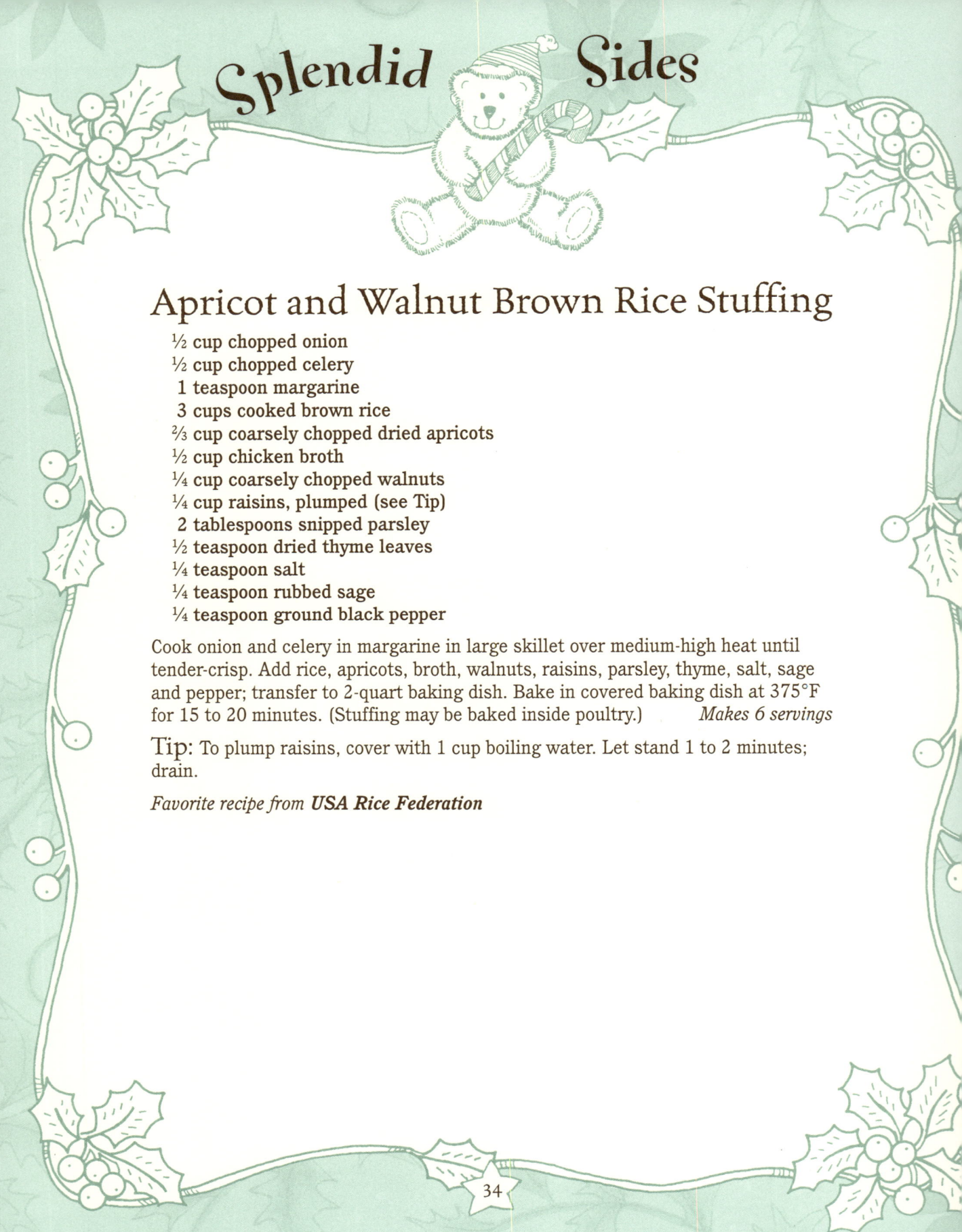

Apricot and Walnut Brown Rice Stuffing

½ cup chopped onion
½ cup chopped celery
 1 teaspoon margarine
 3 cups cooked brown rice
⅔ cup coarsely chopped dried apricots
½ cup chicken broth
¼ cup coarsely chopped walnuts
¼ cup raisins, plumped (see Tip)
 2 tablespoons snipped parsley
½ teaspoon dried thyme leaves
¼ teaspoon salt
¼ teaspoon rubbed sage
¼ teaspoon ground black pepper

Cook onion and celery in margarine in large skillet over medium-high heat until tender-crisp. Add rice, apricots, broth, walnuts, raisins, parsley, thyme, salt, sage and pepper; transfer to 2-quart baking dish. Bake in covered baking dish at 375°F for 15 to 20 minutes. (Stuffing may be baked inside poultry.)   *Makes 6 servings*

Tip: To plump raisins, cover with 1 cup boiling water. Let stand 1 to 2 minutes; drain.

Favorite recipe from **USA Rice Federation**

Cranberry Salad

2 cups cranberries
1 cup water
1 cup EQUAL® SPOONFUL*
1 small package cranberry or cherry sugar-free gelatin
1 cup boiling water
1 cup diced celery
1 can (7¼ ounces) crushed pineapple, undrained
½ cup chopped walnuts

*May substitute 24 packets Equal® sweetener.

● Bring cranberries and 1 cup water to a boil. Remove from heat when cranberries have popped open. Add Equal® and stir. Set aside to cool.

● Dissolve gelatin with 1 cup boiling water. Add cranberry sauce; mix thoroughly. Add celery, pineapple and walnuts. Pour into mold or bowl. Place in refrigerator until set.

Makes 8 servings

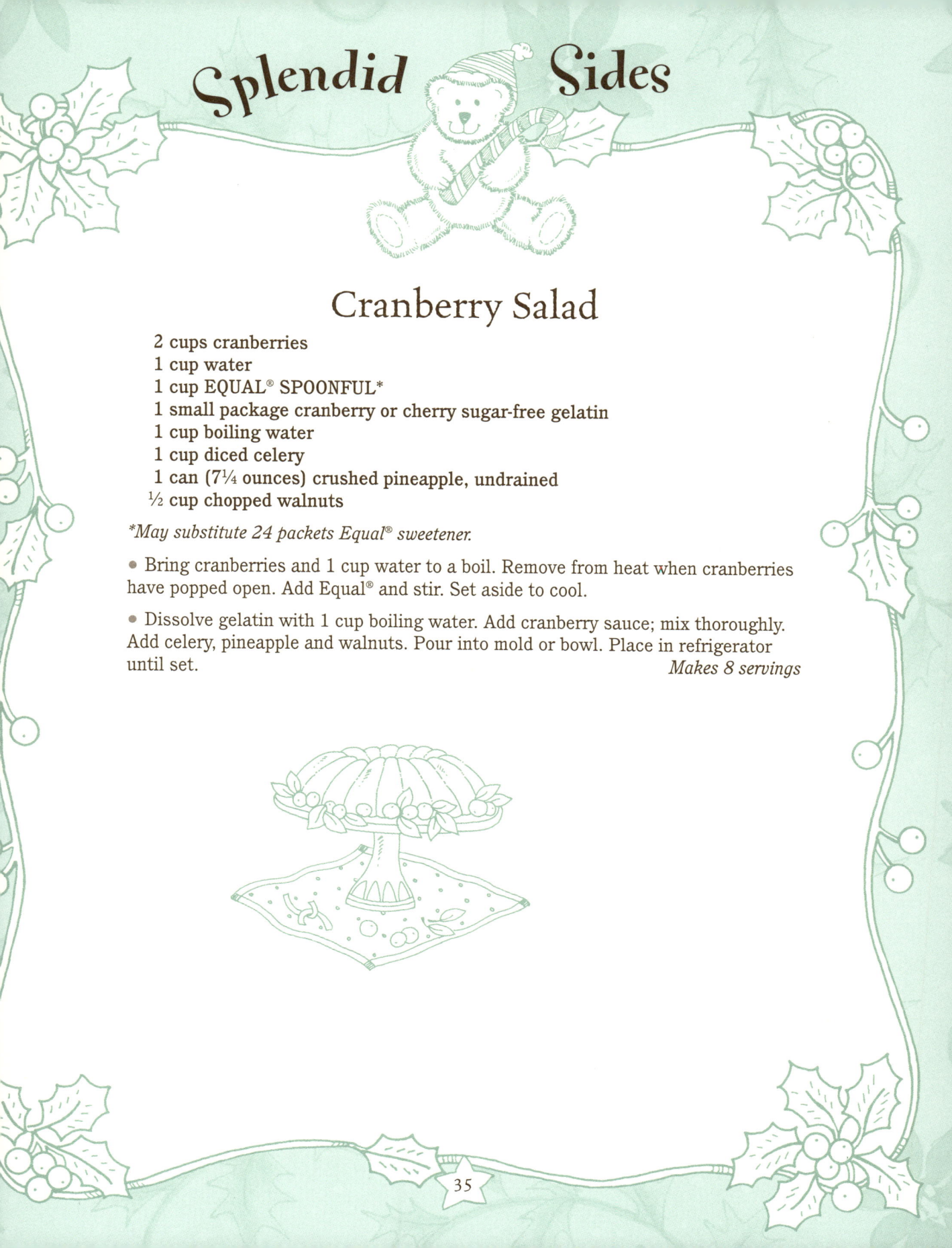

Sweet Potato and Apple Casserole

1 sheet (24×18 inches) heavy-duty foil, generously sprayed with nonstick
    cooking spray
½ cup packed dark brown sugar
½ teaspoon ground cinnamon
¼ teaspoon ground mace or nutmeg
2 pounds sweet potatoes, peeled, sliced in half lengthwise and cut crosswise
    into ½-inch slices
    Salt
3 tablespoons butter, divided
2 Granny Smith apples, peeled, cored and quartered
½ cup granola cereal

1. Preheat oven to 375°F. Place foil loosely in 8×8-inch or 9×9-inch baking pan.

2. Mix brown sugar, cinnamon and mace in small bowl. Place ⅓ of potato slices
in center of foil sheet. Sprinkle with salt to taste. Crumble half the sugar mixture
over potatoes and dot with 1 tablespoon butter.

3. Slice each apple quarter into four wedges. Layer half the apples on top of potatoes.
Repeat layers using potatoes, sugar mixture, butter and apples. Top with remaining
potatoes and 1 tablespoon butter.

4. Double fold sides and ends of foil to seal packet, leaving head space for heat
circulation.

5. Bake in baking pan 25 minutes. Remove from oven. Carefully open one end
of packet to allow steam to escape. Open top of packet; spoon liquid in bottom of
packet over potatoes. Sprinkle with granola; do not reseal packet. Bake 35 minutes
more or until potatoes are fork-tender. *Makes 6 servings*

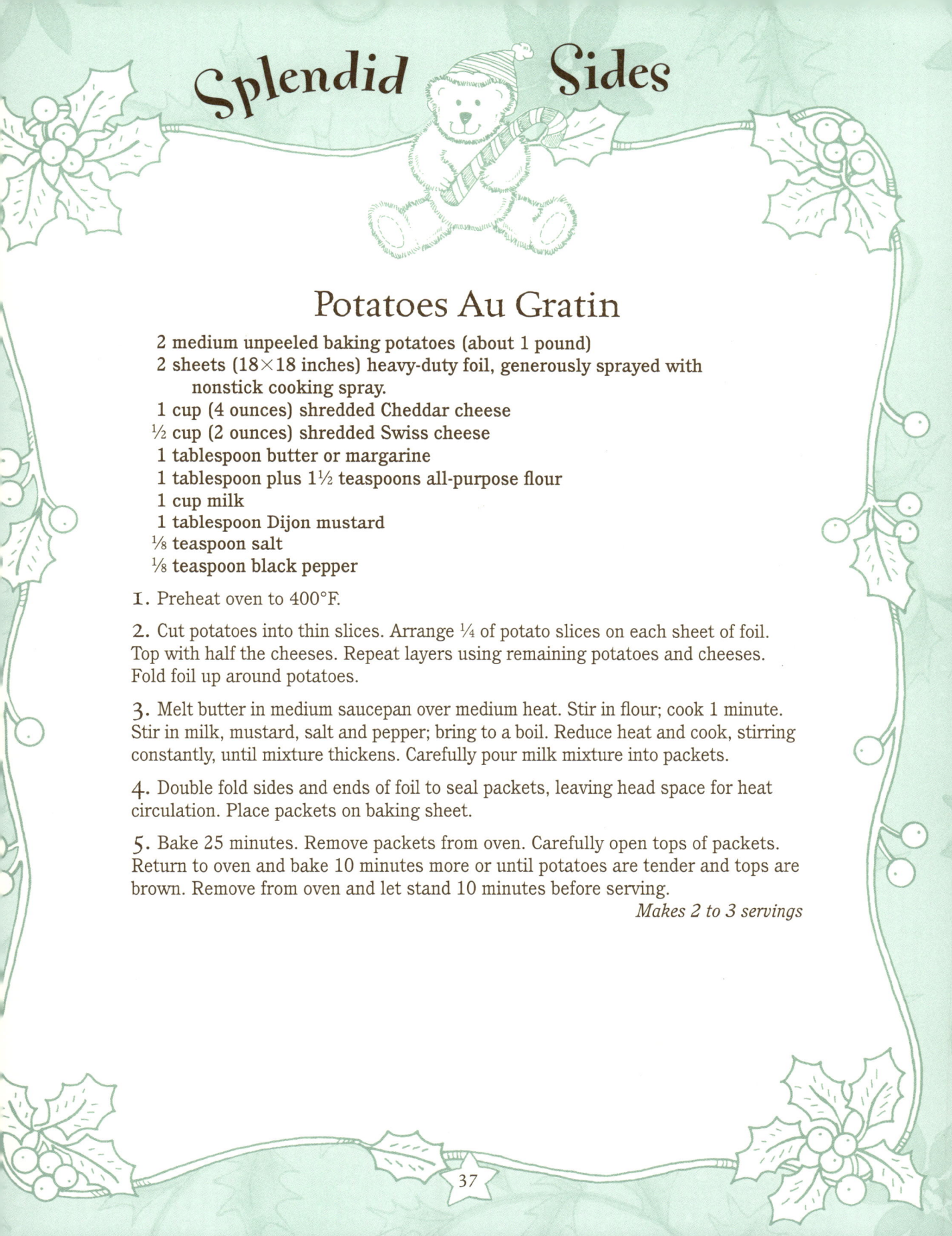

Potatoes Au Gratin

2 medium unpeeled baking potatoes (about 1 pound)
2 sheets (18×18 inches) heavy-duty foil, generously sprayed with
    nonstick cooking spray.
1 cup (4 ounces) shredded Cheddar cheese
½ cup (2 ounces) shredded Swiss cheese
1 tablespoon butter or margarine
1 tablespoon plus 1½ teaspoons all-purpose flour
1 cup milk
1 tablespoon Dijon mustard
⅛ teaspoon salt
⅛ teaspoon black pepper

1. Preheat oven to 400°F.

2. Cut potatoes into thin slices. Arrange ¼ of potato slices on each sheet of foil. Top with half the cheeses. Repeat layers using remaining potatoes and cheeses. Fold foil up around potatoes.

3. Melt butter in medium saucepan over medium heat. Stir in flour; cook 1 minute. Stir in milk, mustard, salt and pepper; bring to a boil. Reduce heat and cook, stirring constantly, until mixture thickens. Carefully pour milk mixture into packets.

4. Double fold sides and ends of foil to seal packets, leaving head space for heat circulation. Place packets on baking sheet.

5. Bake 25 minutes. Remove packets from oven. Carefully open tops of packets. Return to oven and bake 10 minutes more or until potatoes are tender and tops are brown. Remove from oven and let stand 10 minutes before serving.

Makes 2 to 3 servings

Old-Fashioned Herb Stuffing

6 slices (8 ounces) whole wheat, rye or white bread (or combination),
    cut into ½-inch cubes
1 tablespoon margarine or butter
1 cup chopped onion
½ cup thinly sliced celery
½ cup thinly sliced carrot
1 cup canned fat-free reduced-sodium chicken broth
1 tablespoon chopped fresh thyme *or* 1 teaspoon dried thyme leaves
1 tablespoon chopped fresh sage *or* 1 teaspoon dried sage leaves
½ teaspoon paprika
¼ teaspoon black pepper

1. Preheat oven to 350°F. Place bread cubes on baking sheet; bake 10 minutes or until dry.

2. Melt margarine in large saucepan over medium heat. Add onion, celery and carrot; cover and cook 10 minutes or until vegetables are tender. Add broth, thyme, sage, paprika and pepper; bring to a simmer. Stir in bread pieces; mix well. Remove pan from heat; set aside.

3. Coat 1½-quart baking dish with nonstick cooking spray. Spoon stuffing into dish. Cover and bake 25 to 30 minutes or until heated through.

Makes 4 servings

Baked Spiced Squash

2 boxes (10 ounces each) BIRDS EYE® frozen Cooked Winter Squash, thawed
2 egg whites, lightly beaten
¼ cup brown sugar
2 teaspoons butter or margarine, melted
1 teaspoon ground cinnamon
½ cup herbed croutons, coarsely crushed

• Preheat oven to 400°F. Combine squash, egg whites, sugar, butter and cinnamon; mix well.

• Pour into 1-quart baking dish sprayed with nonstick cooking spray.

• Bake 20 to 25 minutes or until center is set.

• Remove from oven; sprinkle crushed croutons on top. Bake 5 to 7 minutes longer or until croutons are browned.   *Makes 6 to 8 servings*

Prep Time: 5 minutes
Cook Time: 25 to 35 minutes

Lemony Steamed Broccoli

1 pound broccoli
1 tablespoon butter
2 teaspoons lemon juice
  Salt and black pepper

1. Break broccoli into florets. Discard large stems. Trim smaller stems; cut stems into thin slices.

2. Place 2 to 3 inches of water and steamer basket in large saucepan; bring water to a boil.

3. Add broccoli; cover. Steam 6 minutes or until crisp-tender.

4. Place broccoli in serving bowl. Add butter and lemon juice; toss lightly to coat. Season with salt and pepper to taste.   *Makes 4 servings*

Glazed Carrots

1 tablespoon butter
1 package (16 ounces) baby carrots
¾ cup apple juice
2 teaspoons honey
1 teaspoon apple cider vinegar
  Salt and pepper

1. Melt butter in medium skillet over medium-high heat. Add carrots; cook and stir until carrots just begin to brown, about 7 to 8 minutes.

2. Add apple juice, honey and vinegar; bring mixture to a boil. Reduce heat to medium and cook 15 minutes or until carrots are tender and liquid is reduced to glaze, stirring occasionally.

3. Season to taste with salt and pepper.   *Makes 4 servings*

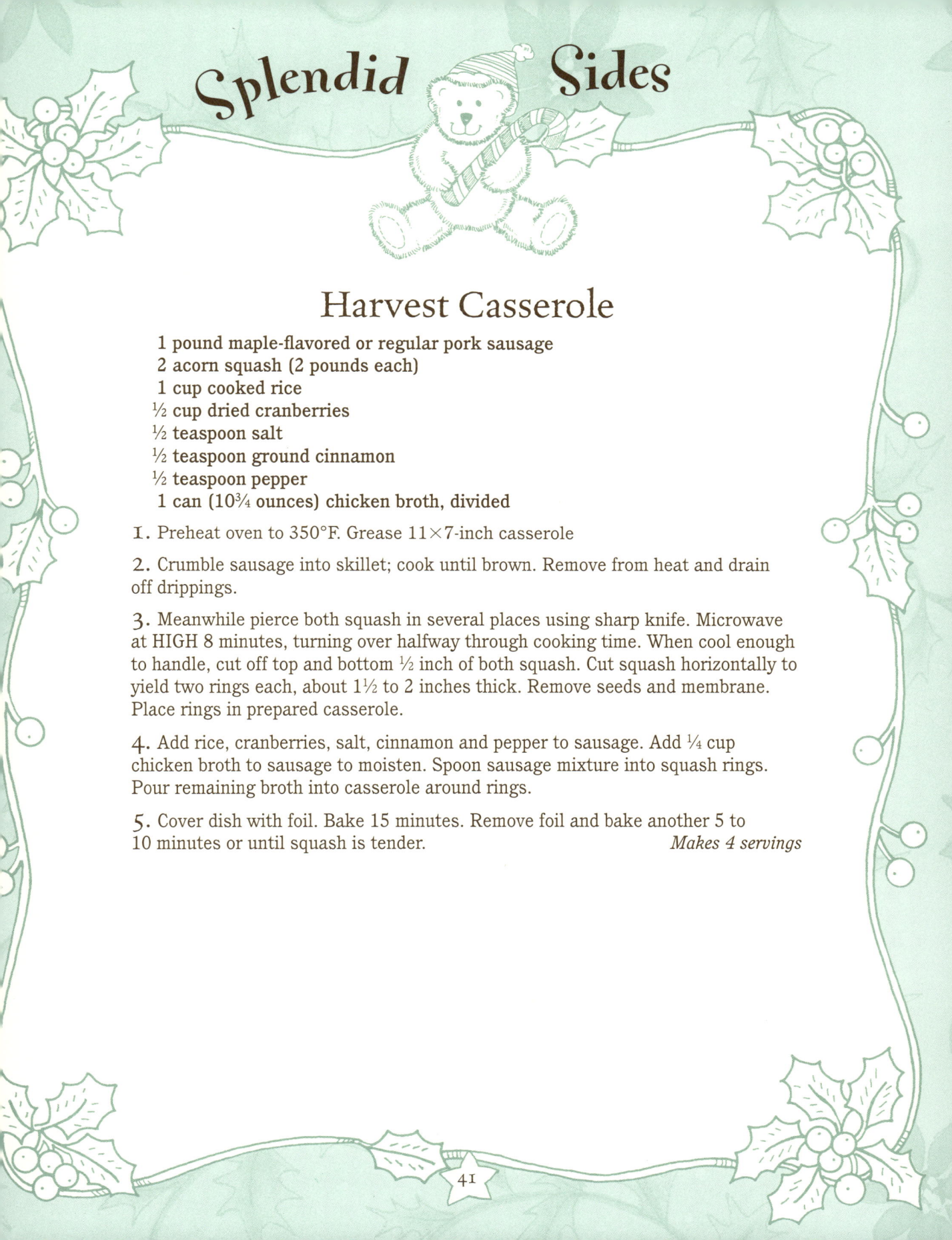

Harvest Casserole

  1 pound maple-flavored or regular pork sausage
  2 acorn squash (2 pounds each)
  1 cup cooked rice
  ½ cup dried cranberries
  ½ teaspoon salt
  ½ teaspoon ground cinnamon
  ½ teaspoon pepper
  1 can (10¾ ounces) chicken broth, divided

1. Preheat oven to 350°F. Grease 11×7-inch casserole

2. Crumble sausage into skillet; cook until brown. Remove from heat and drain off drippings.

3. Meanwhile pierce both squash in several places using sharp knife. Microwave at HIGH 8 minutes, turning over halfway through cooking time. When cool enough to handle, cut off top and bottom ½ inch of both squash. Cut squash horizontally to yield two rings each, about 1½ to 2 inches thick. Remove seeds and membrane. Place rings in prepared casserole.

4. Add rice, cranberries, salt, cinnamon and pepper to sausage. Add ¼ cup chicken broth to sausage to moisten. Spoon sausage mixture into squash rings. Pour remaining broth into casserole around rings.

5. Cover dish with foil. Bake 15 minutes. Remove foil and bake another 5 to 10 minutes or until squash is tender.   *Makes 4 servings*

Fall Cranberry Nut Squash

2 medium acorn squash
½ cup packed light brown sugar
⅓ cup PETER PAN® Honey Roasted Creamy Peanut Butter
2 tablespoons butter
1 teaspoon finely shredded fresh orange peel
1 teaspoon vanilla
¼ teaspoon ground cinnamon
¼ teaspoon ground allspice
½ cup dried cranberries

Preheat oven to 350°F. Cut off ends of squash, then cut horizontally into halves; remove seeds. Place halves, cut sides up, in 11×7×2-inch baking pan. In bowl, stir together sugar, peanut butter, butter, orange peel, vanilla, cinnamon and allspice. Spoon mixture into and onto squash halves. Bake, covered, 30 minutes. Sprinkle 2 tablespoons cranberries over each squash half. Bake, uncovered, 10 to 15 minutes or until squash are tender. *Makes 4 servings*

Preparation Time: 7 minutes
Cooking Time: 45 minutes

Grandma's Old Fashioned Sausage Stuffing

1 pound BOB EVANS® Original Recipe or Sage Roll Sausage
4 large apples, such as Red Delicious, McIntosh or Granny Smith
½ cup chopped celery
2 teaspoons salt
8 cups dried, toasted fresh or prepared seasoned bread cubes
1 small minced onion (optional)
½ cup milk
   Canned chicken broth (optional)

Crumble sausage into medium skillet. Cook over medium heat until lightly browned, stirring occasionally. Place sausage and drippings in large bowl. Core, peel and chop apples into ½-inch pieces. Add apples and all remaining ingredients except broth to sausage mixture; blend thoroughly. Bake loosely stuffed in bird or place stuffing in greased 13×9-inch baking dish. Add turkey drippings and/or broth to adjust moistness and bake 30 to 45 minutes in 350°F oven. Leftover stuffing should be removed from bird and stored in the refrigerator separately. Reheat thoroughly before serving.   *Makes 10 side-dish servings, enough for a 12- to 15-pound turkey*

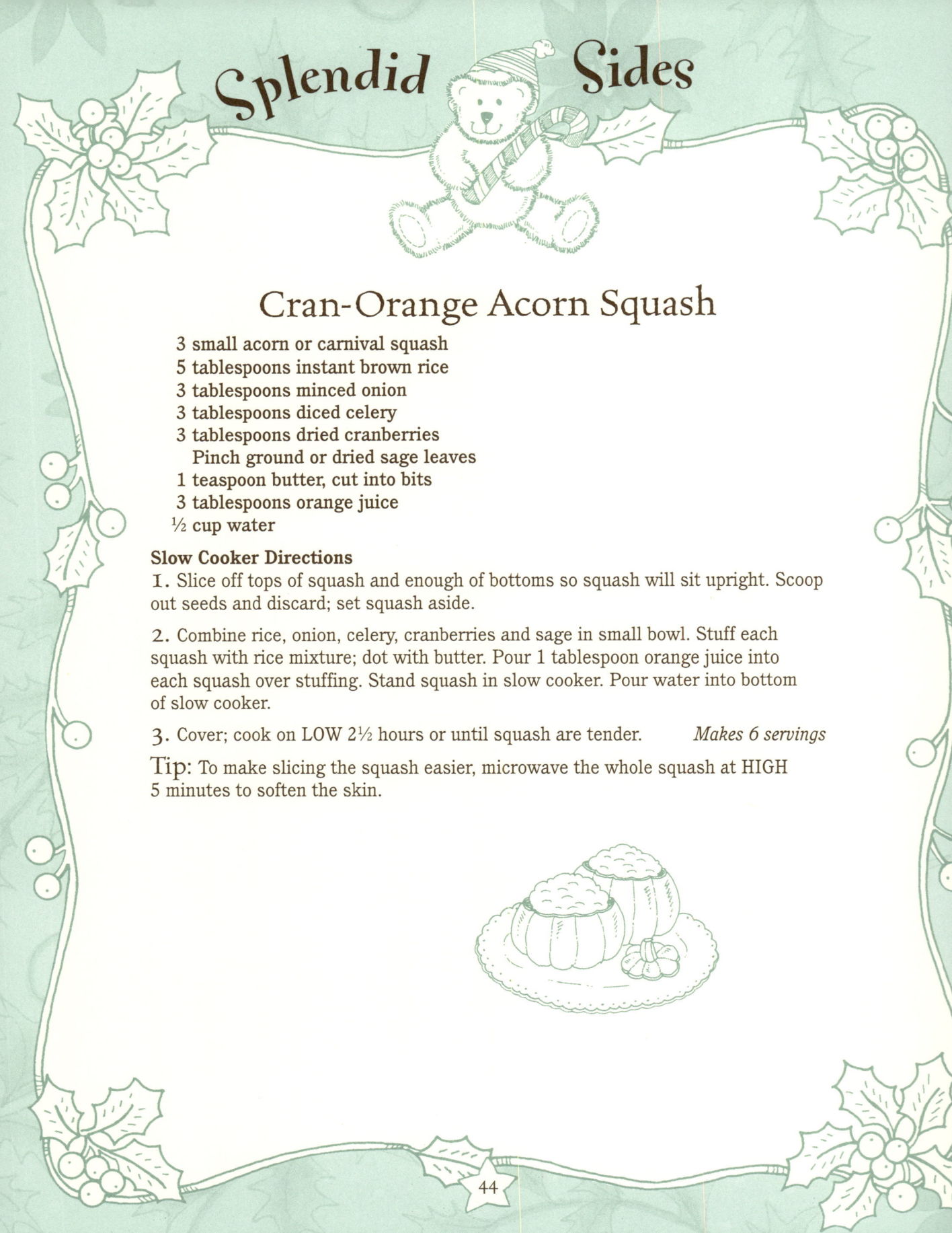

Cran-Orange Acorn Squash

3 small acorn or carnival squash
5 tablespoons instant brown rice
3 tablespoons minced onion
3 tablespoons diced celery
3 tablespoons dried cranberries
 Pinch ground or dried sage leaves
1 teaspoon butter, cut into bits
3 tablespoons orange juice
½ cup water

Slow Cooker Directions

1. Slice off tops of squash and enough of bottoms so squash will sit upright. Scoop out seeds and discard; set squash aside.

2. Combine rice, onion, celery, cranberries and sage in small bowl. Stuff each squash with rice mixture; dot with butter. Pour 1 tablespoon orange juice into each squash over stuffing. Stand squash in slow cooker. Pour water into bottom of slow cooker.

3. Cover; cook on LOW 2½ hours or until squash are tender.   *Makes 6 servings*

Tip: To make slicing the squash easier, microwave the whole squash at HIGH 5 minutes to soften the skin.

Garden Vegetable Rice Medley

   1 cup water
1½ cups DOLE® Peeled Mini Carrots
   1 cup DOLE® Broccoli or Cauliflower florets
   1 cup DOLE® Sugar Peas or Green Beans
   2 medium DOLE® Red, Yellow or Green Bell Peppers, cut into 2-inch pieces
   1 package (8 ounces) mushrooms, stems trimmed
   3 cups hot cooked brown or white rice
   1 cup (4 ounces) shredded low-fat cheddar cheese
   ⅓ cup crumbled feta cheese

● Pour water in large saucepan; heat to boiling. Add carrots and broccoli. Reduce heat to low; cover and cook 5 minutes. Add sugar peas, bell peppers and mushrooms; cook 5 minutes more until vegetables are tender-crisp. Drain vegetables.

● Spoon hot rice onto large serving platter; top with vegetables and cheeses.

● Cover with aluminum foil; let stand 3 minutes or until cheese melts.

Makes 4 servings

Prep Time: 15 minutes
Cook Time: 15 minutes

Lemon Butter Green Beans

1½ teaspoons LAWRY'S® Lemon Pepper
 ½ cup melted butter or margarine
 1 package (16 ounces) frozen green beans, cooked according to package
    directions and drained

In small bowl, combine Lemon Pepper and butter; mix well. Pour over hot green beans right before serving. *Makes 6 servings*

Variations: Prepare beans in microwave for even shorter cooking time. Try other vegetables such as corn, broccoli, and your favorite combinations for variety!

Prep. Time: 5 minutes
Cook Time: 5 to 10 minutes

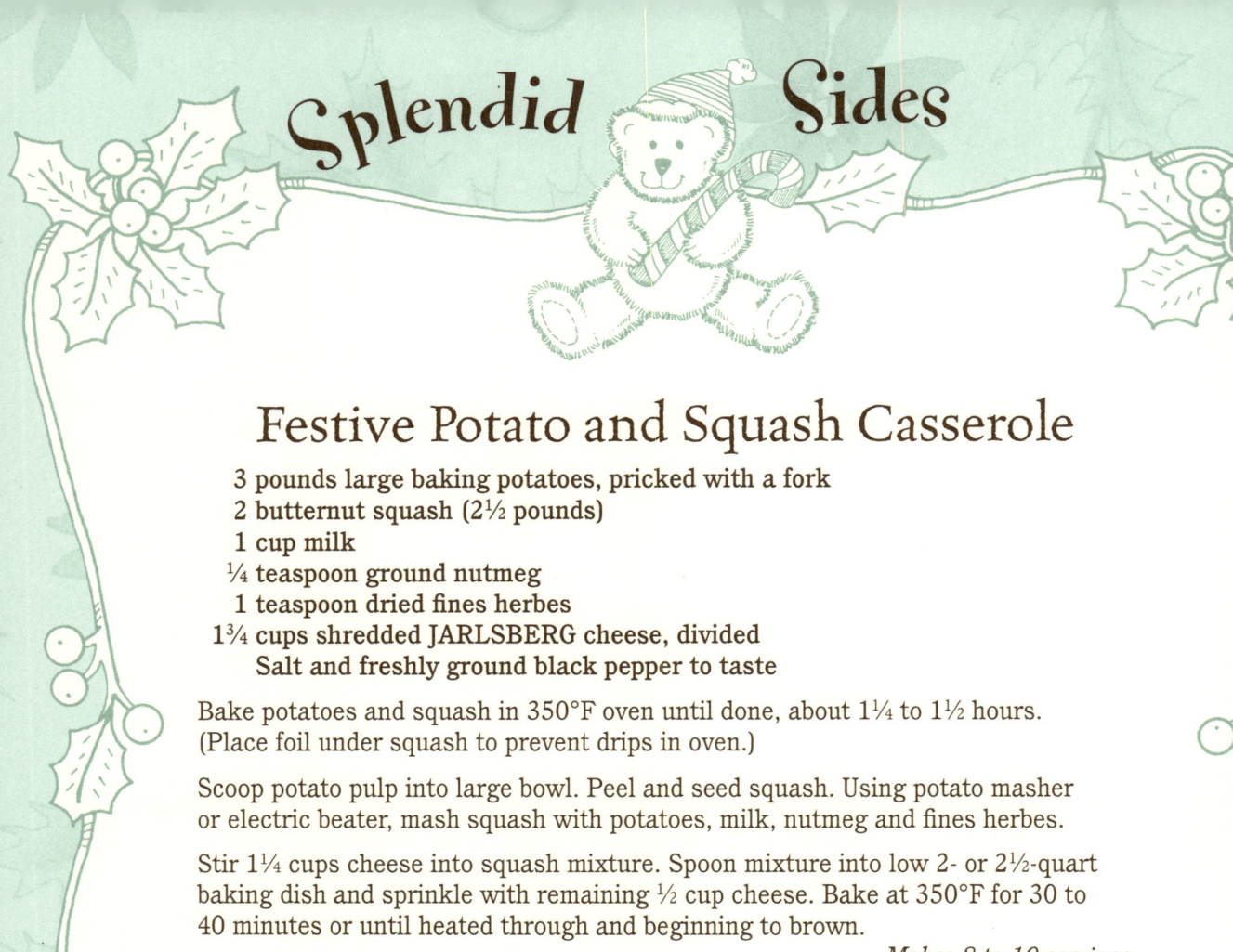

Festive Potato and Squash Casserole

3 pounds large baking potatoes, pricked with a fork
2 butternut squash (2½ pounds)
1 cup milk
¼ teaspoon ground nutmeg
1 teaspoon dried fines herbes
1¾ cups shredded JARLSBERG cheese, divided
Salt and freshly ground black pepper to taste

Bake potatoes and squash in 350°F oven until done, about 1¼ to 1½ hours. (Place foil under squash to prevent drips in oven.)

Scoop potato pulp into large bowl. Peel and seed squash. Using potato masher or electric beater, mash squash with potatoes, milk, nutmeg and fines herbes.

Stir 1¼ cups cheese into squash mixture. Spoon mixture into low 2- or 2½-quart baking dish and sprinkle with remaining ½ cup cheese. Bake at 350°F for 30 to 40 minutes or until heated through and beginning to brown.

Makes 8 to 10 servings

Splendid Sides

Green Beans with Toasted Pecans

    3 tablespoons I CAN'T BELIEVE IT'S NOT BUTTER!® Spread, melted
    1 teaspoon sugar
    ¼ teaspoon garlic powder
        Pinch ground red pepper
        Salt to taste
    ⅓ cup chopped pecans
    1 pound green beans

In small bowl, blend I Can't Believe It's Not Butter!® Spread, sugar, garlic powder, pepper and salt.

In 12-inch nonstick skillet, heat 2 teaspoons garlic mixture over medium-high heat and cook pecans, stirring frequently, 2 minutes or until pecans are golden. Remove pecans and set aside.

In same skillet, heat remaining garlic mixture and stir in green beans. Cook, covered, over medium heat, stirring occasionally, 6 minutes or until green beans are tender. Stir in pecans. *Makes 4 servings*

Nutty Vegetable Pilaf

1 tablespoon vegetable oil
2 cups coarsely chopped broccoli
2 medium carrots, julienned
1 medium onion, chopped
1 cup sliced fresh mushrooms
2 cloves garlic, minced
½ teaspoon dried thyme leaves
½ teaspoon dried basil leaves
½ teaspoon salt
¼ teaspoon ground black pepper
3 cups cooked brown rice (cooked in low-sodium chicken broth*)
½ cup chopped pecans, toasted**
½ cup grated Parmesan cheese (optional)

For a vegetarian entree, cook brown rice in vegetable broth.

**To toast pecans, place on baking sheet; bake 5 to 7 minutes in 350° oven, or until nuts are just beginning to darken and are fragrant.*

Heat oil in large skillet over medium-high heat until hot. Add broccoli, carrots and onion. Cook and stir 5 to 7 minutes or until broccoli and carrots are tender and onion is beginning to brown. Add mushrooms, garlic, thyme, basil, salt and pepper. Cook and stir 2 to 3 minutes or until mushrooms are tender. Add rice and pecans; cook 1 to 2 minutes, stirring, until well blended and thoroughly heated. Just before serving sprinkle with cheese, if desired.   *Makes 6 servings*

Favorite recipe from **USA Rice Federation**

Splendid Sides

Garlic Mashed Potatoes

1½ pounds DOLE® Russet or White Potatoes, peeled, cut into ½-inch cubes
5 large cloves garlic, peeled
1½ teaspoons salt, divided
½ cup buttermilk
2 teaspoons butter or margarine
¼ teaspoon black pepper

• Cover potatoes, garlic and 1 teaspoon salt with water in large saucepan. Heat to boiling; reduce heat to low and continue cooking 10 to 15 minutes or until potatoes are very tender. Drain.

• Combine potato mixture, buttermilk, butter, remaining ½ teaspoon salt and pepper in large mixer bowl. Beat until smooth. *Makes 4 servings*

Blue Cheese Mashed Potatoes: Omit garlic cloves. In step 2, add ¼ cup crumbled blue cheese with buttermilk to potato mixture.

Prep Time: 15 minutes
Cook Time: 15 minutes

Pine Nut Rice Dressing

1 bag SUCCESS® White or Brown Rice
⅓ cup chopped onion
⅓ cup chopped celery
1 tablespoon margarine
¼ cup pine nuts
1 tablespoon chopped fresh parsley
¾ teaspoon poultry seasoning
½ teaspoon black pepper
¼ teaspoon salt
¼ cup chopped green onions
¼ cup chicken stock

Prepare rice according to package directions.

Meanwhile, cook and stir onion and celery in margarine. Add pine nuts, parsley, poultry seasoning, pepper and salt. Fold in cooked rice. Add green onions and chicken stock.   *Makes 4 servings*

Broccoli Casserole

1 package (about 6 ounces) stuffing mix
1 can (10¾ ounces) condensed cream of mushroom soup, undiluted
1 package (10 ounces) frozen chopped broccoli, thawed
½ small onion, chopped
½ cup (2 ounces) shredded mozzarella cheese

1. Preheat oven to 350°F. Grease 2-quart casserole.

2. Prepare stuffing mix according to package directions. Add soup, broccoli, and onion; mix well. Pour into prepared dish. Cover with cheese.

3. Bake 30 minutes or until heated through and cheese melts.

Makes 4 servings

Cranberry-Raisin Stuffing

12 slices cinnamon-raisin bread, toasted
½ cup (1 stick) butter or margarine
2½ cups chopped onions
1 teaspoon rubbed sage
1 bag (12 ounces) fresh or partially thawed frozen cranberries, washed, picked through and coarsely chopped
¼ cup sugar
¼ to ½ cup chicken broth*

If baking stuffing in casserole dish, use ½ cup chicken broth and bake, covered, at 350°F for 45 minutes or until heated through.

1. Cut toast into ½-inch cubes. Place in large bowl; set aside. Melt butter in large skillet; add onions. Cook and stir about 10 minutes or until tender. Add sage; cook 1 minute more.

2. Toss cranberries with sugar in medium bowl. Add onion mixture and cranberries to bread cubes; mix well. Pour ¼ cup chicken broth over bread cube mixture; mix until evenly moistened. Stuff body and neck of turkey and cook according to instructions given with turkey.   *Makes 7½ cups stuffing*

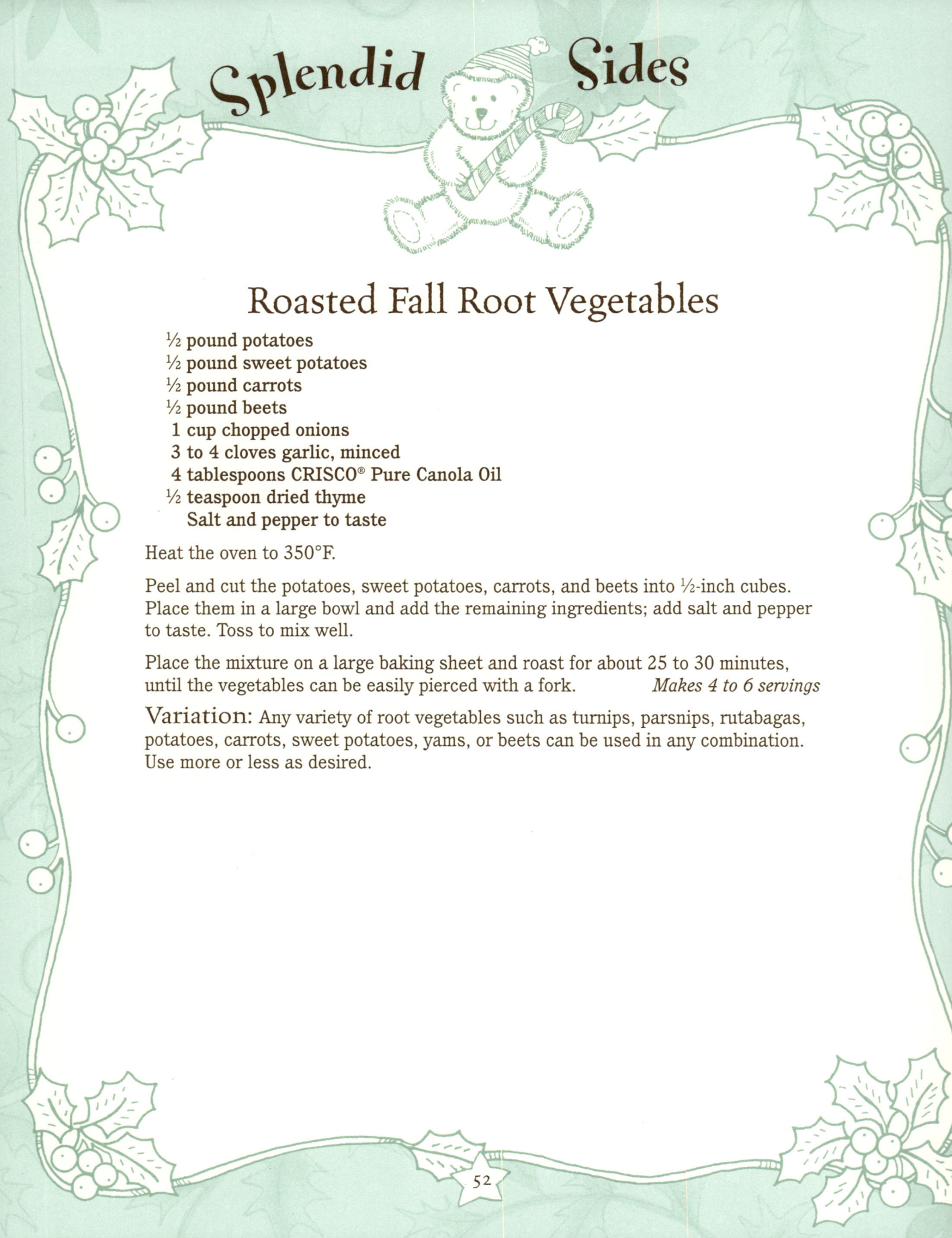

Roasted Fall Root Vegetables

½ pound potatoes
½ pound sweet potatoes
½ pound carrots
½ pound beets
1 cup chopped onions
3 to 4 cloves garlic, minced
4 tablespoons CRISCO® Pure Canola Oil
½ teaspoon dried thyme
  Salt and pepper to taste

Heat the oven to 350°F.

Peel and cut the potatoes, sweet potatoes, carrots, and beets into ½-inch cubes. Place them in a large bowl and add the remaining ingredients; add salt and pepper to taste. Toss to mix well.

Place the mixture on a large baking sheet and roast for about 25 to 30 minutes, until the vegetables can be easily pierced with a fork.   *Makes 4 to 6 servings*

Variation: Any variety of root vegetables such as turnips, parsnips, rutabagas, potatoes, carrots, sweet potatoes, yams, or beets can be used in any combination. Use more or less as desired.

Splendid Sides

Vegetable Casserole

1 package (about 16 ounces) frozen spinach
¾ cup (1½ sticks) unsalted butter, divided
   Salt
   Black pepper
8 potatoes, peeled and cooked until tender
1 cup milk
1 pound carrots, sliced and cooked until tender
1 pound green beans, cut into 1-inch pieces and cooked until tender
½ teaspoon paprika

1. Preheat oven to 375°F. Lightly grease 4-quart casserole or roasting pan.

2. Cook spinach according to package directions; drain. Spread spinach in prepared casserole; dot with 1 tablespoon butter and season with salt and pepper.

3. Mash potatoes with milk and ½ cup butter until creamy.

4. Layer half of potatoes, carrots and beans over spinach. Dot with another 1 tablespoon butter; season with salt and pepper.

5. Top with remaining potatoes. Dot with remaining 2 tablespoons butter and sprinkle with paprika. Bake 1 hour or until heated through and lightly browned.

Makes 10 to 12 servings

Delicious Corn Soufflé

2 eggs
2 egg whites
3 tablespoons all-purpose flour
1 tablespoon sugar
½ teaspoon black pepper
1 can (16½ ounces) cream-style corn
2 cups fresh corn kernels or frozen corn, thawed and drained
1 cup (4 ounces) shredded Mexican cheese blend or Monterey Jack cheese
1 jar (2 ounces) chopped pimientos, drained
⅓ cup milk
Fresh parsley (optional)

1. Preheat oven to 350°F. Spray 8-inch round baking dish with nonstick cooking spray. Place dish in oven.

2. Combine eggs, egg whites, flour, sugar and pepper in large bowl; beat at high speed of electric mixer until smooth. Stir in creamed corn, corn kernels, cheese, pimientos and milk. Pour into hot baking dish.

3. Bake, uncovered, 55 minutes or until set. Let stand 15 minutes before serving. Garnish with parsley, if desired. *Makes 6 servings*

Fruited Wild Rice with Toasted Nuts

  2 boxes (6.2 ounces each) fast-cooking long-grain and wild rice
  2 tablespoons walnut or vegetable oil, divided
  1 package (2½ ounces) walnut pieces *or* ⅔ cup slivered almonds
  1 package (2¼ ounces) pecan pieces
  2 cups chopped onions
 12 dried apricots, sliced (about ½ cup)
  ½ cup dried cherries or dried cranberries
  2 teaspoons minced fresh ginger
  ¼ teaspoon red pepper flakes
  ¼ cup honey
  3 tablespoons soy sauce
  1 tablespoon grated orange peel

1. Cook rice according to package directions.

2. Meanwhile, heat 1 tablespoon oil in large nonstick skillet or wok over medium-high heat 1 minute. Add walnuts and pecans; cook, stirring frequently, 8 minutes or until pecans are browned. Remove from skillet and set aside.

3. Add remaining 1 tablespoon oil and onions to skillet; cook 10 minutes or until onions begin to brown. Add apricots, cherries, ginger, red pepper flakes and reserved nuts; cook 5 minutes.

4. Whisk together honey, soy sauce and orange peel in small bowl; add to onion mixture. Toss with rice.   *Makes 4 servings*

Note: This dish can be served as a chilled rice salad. Spoon hot cooked rice evenly on large baking sheet to cool quickly, about 8 to 10 minutes. Toss with cooled nuts, onion mixture and honey mixture.

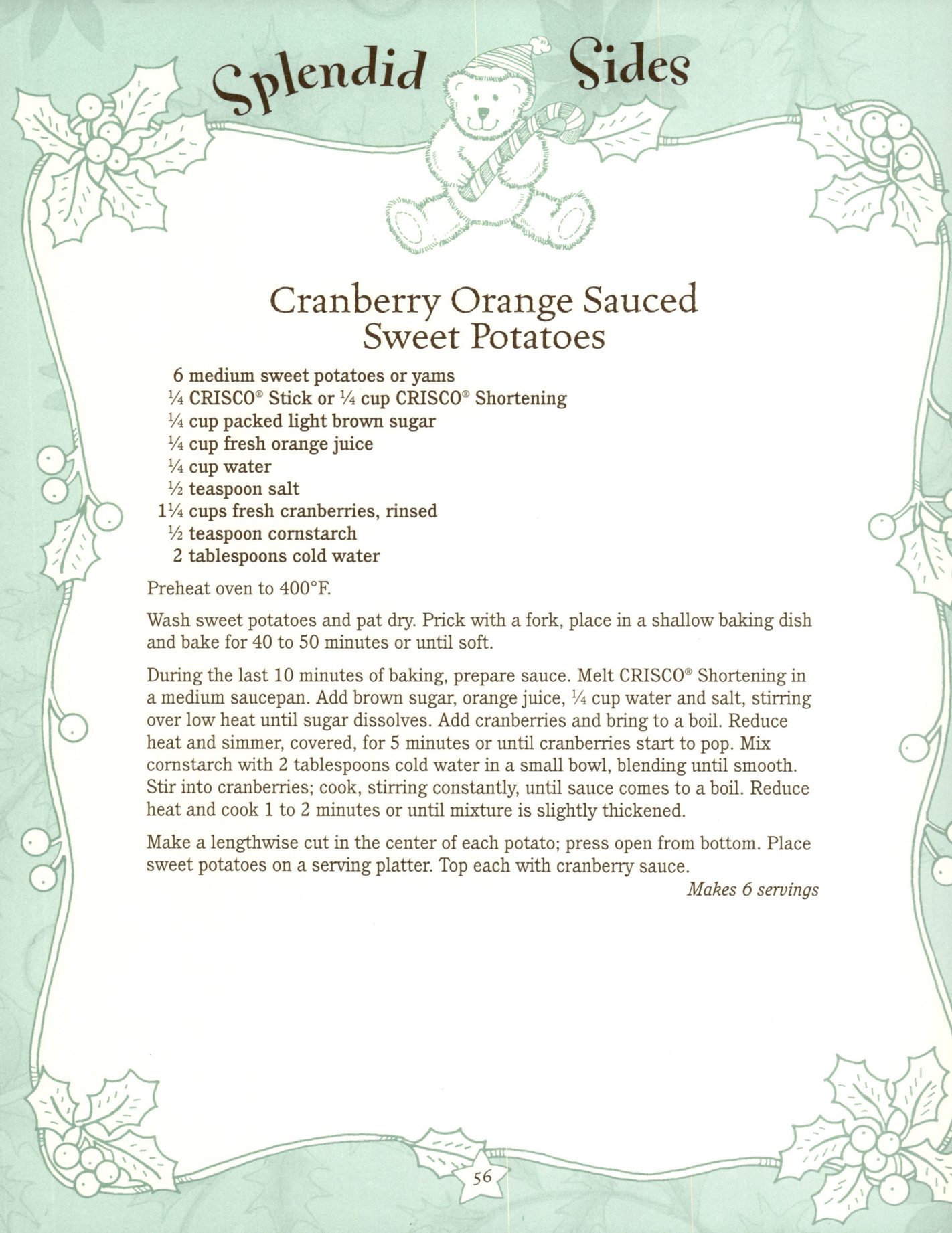

Cranberry Orange Sauced
Sweet Potatoes

  6 medium sweet potatoes or yams
  ¼ CRISCO® Stick or ¼ cup CRISCO® Shortening
  ¼ cup packed light brown sugar
  ¼ cup fresh orange juice
  ¼ cup water
  ½ teaspoon salt
1¼ cups fresh cranberries, rinsed
  ½ teaspoon cornstarch
  2 tablespoons cold water

Preheat oven to 400°F.

Wash sweet potatoes and pat dry. Prick with a fork, place in a shallow baking dish and bake for 40 to 50 minutes or until soft.

During the last 10 minutes of baking, prepare sauce. Melt CRISCO® Shortening in a medium saucepan. Add brown sugar, orange juice, ¼ cup water and salt, stirring over low heat until sugar dissolves. Add cranberries and bring to a boil. Reduce heat and simmer, covered, for 5 minutes or until cranberries start to pop. Mix cornstarch with 2 tablespoons cold water in a small bowl, blending until smooth. Stir into cranberries; cook, stirring constantly, until sauce comes to a boil. Reduce heat and cook 1 to 2 minutes or until mixture is slightly thickened.

Make a lengthwise cut in the center of each potato; press open from bottom. Place sweet potatoes on a serving platter. Top each with cranberry sauce.

Makes 6 servings

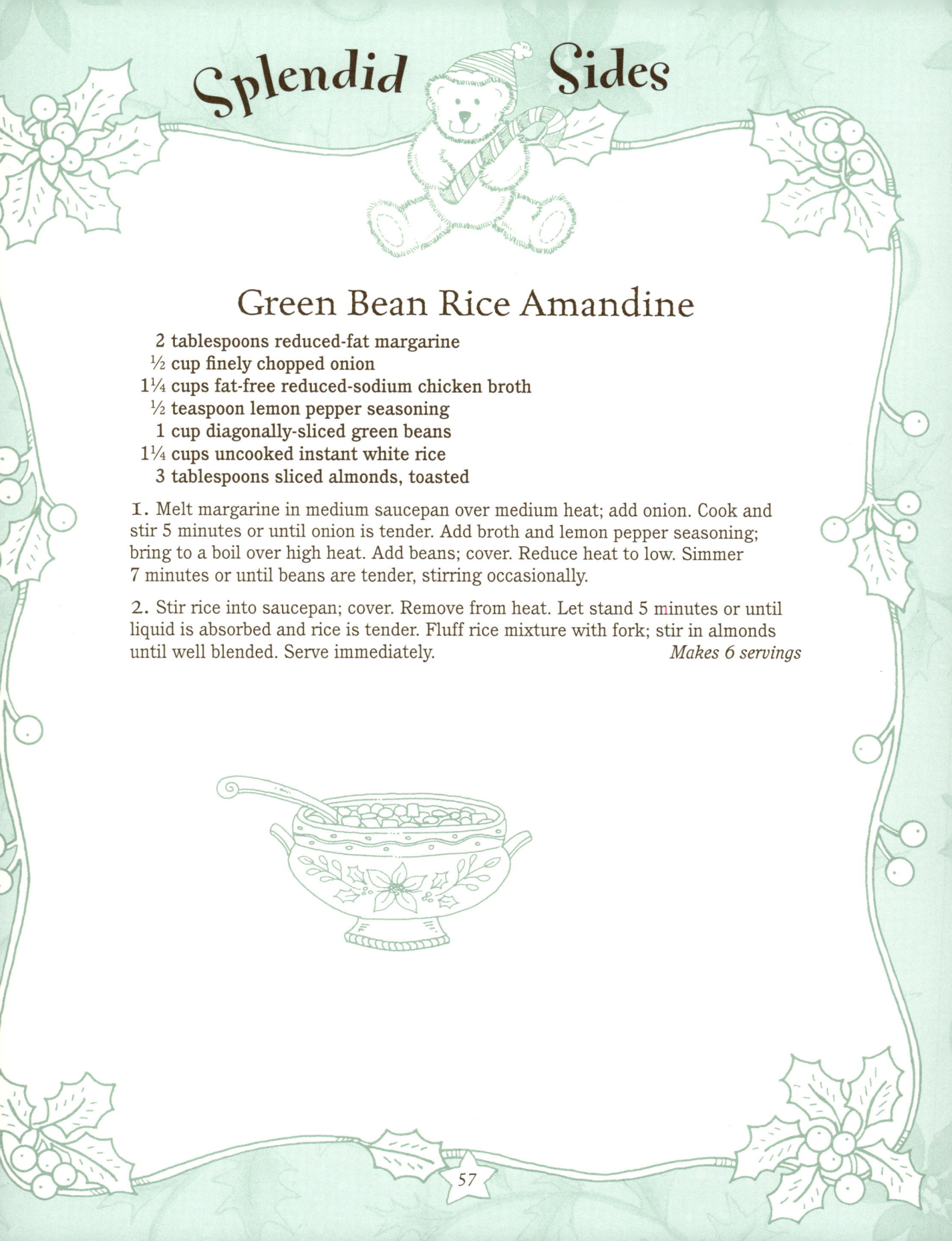

Green Bean Rice Amandine

2 tablespoons reduced-fat margarine
½ cup finely chopped onion
1¼ cups fat-free reduced-sodium chicken broth
½ teaspoon lemon pepper seasoning
1 cup diagonally-sliced green beans
1¼ cups uncooked instant white rice
3 tablespoons sliced almonds, toasted

1. Melt margarine in medium saucepan over medium heat; add onion. Cook and stir 5 minutes or until onion is tender. Add broth and lemon pepper seasoning; bring to a boil over high heat. Add beans; cover. Reduce heat to low. Simmer 7 minutes or until beans are tender, stirring occasionally.

2. Stir rice into saucepan; cover. Remove from heat. Let stand 5 minutes or until liquid is absorbed and rice is tender. Fluff rice mixture with fork; stir in almonds until well blended. Serve immediately. *Makes 6 servings*

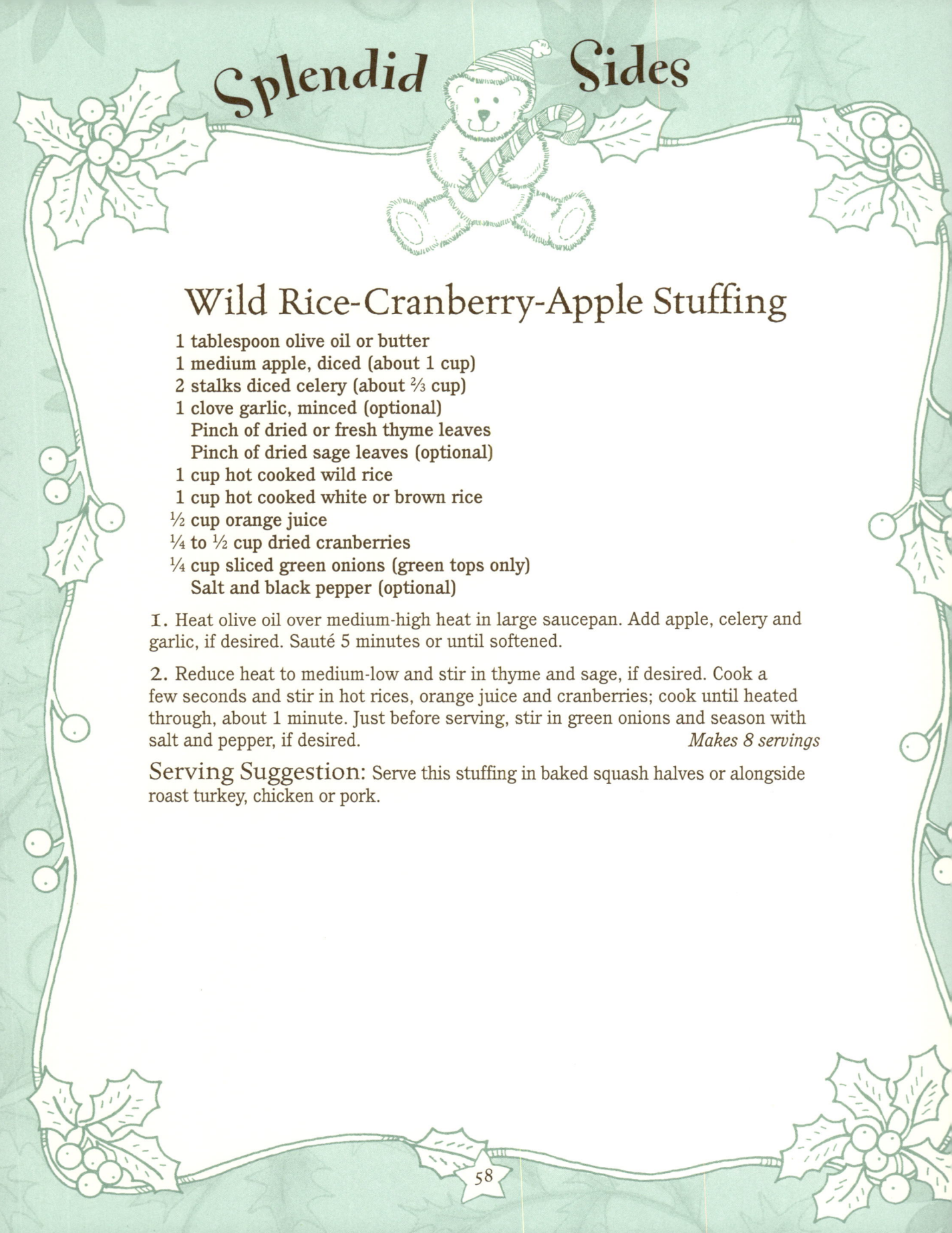

Wild Rice-Cranberry-Apple Stuffing

1 tablespoon olive oil or butter
1 medium apple, diced (about 1 cup)
2 stalks diced celery (about ⅔ cup)
1 clove garlic, minced (optional)
   Pinch of dried or fresh thyme leaves
   Pinch of dried sage leaves (optional)
1 cup hot cooked wild rice
1 cup hot cooked white or brown rice
½ cup orange juice
¼ to ½ cup dried cranberries
¼ cup sliced green onions (green tops only)
   Salt and black pepper (optional)

1. Heat olive oil over medium-high heat in large saucepan. Add apple, celery and garlic, if desired. Sauté 5 minutes or until softened.

2. Reduce heat to medium-low and stir in thyme and sage, if desired. Cook a few seconds and stir in hot rices, orange juice and cranberries; cook until heated through, about 1 minute. Just before serving, stir in green onions and season with salt and pepper, if desired.   *Makes 8 servings*

Serving Suggestion: Serve this stuffing in baked squash halves or alongside roast turkey, chicken or pork.

Broccoli in Cheese Sauce

1 bag (16 ounces) frozen broccoli florets
1 sheet (24×12 inches) heavy-duty foil, lightly sprayed with
    nonstick cooking spray
1 can (10¾ ounces) condensed Cheddar cheese soup
1 medium red or yellow bell pepper, cut into 1-inch pieces
¼ cup chopped onion
¼ cup milk
1½ teaspoons Worcestershire sauce
⅛ teaspoon black pepper

1. Preheat oven to 450°F. Place frozen broccoli in center of sheet of foil. Fold foil up around broccoli to create pan.

2. Combine soup, bell pepper, onion, milk, Worcestershire sauce and black pepper in medium bowl; stir to blend. Pour over broccoli.

3. Double fold sides and ends of foil to seal packet, leaving head space for heat circulation. Place packet on baking sheet.

4. Bake 25 minutes or until vegetables are tender. Remove from oven. Carefully open one end of packet to allow steam to escape. Open packet and transfer broccoli mixture to serving bowl.

Makes 6 servings

Maple Glazed Squash

1 large acorn squash, seeded and cut into quarters
  Butter-flavored vegetable cooking spray
1 large tart cooking apple, unpeeled, cored and sliced
¼ cup raisins
¼ cup chopped walnuts

Maple Flavored Syrup
  1 cup apple juice
2½ teaspoons cornstarch
  1 tablespoon stick butter or margarine
¼ cup EQUAL® SPOONFUL*
  1 teaspoon maple flavoring
  1 teaspoon vanilla

May substitute 6 packets Equal® sweetener.

• Place squash, cut sides up, in baking pan; add ½ cup hot water. Bake, covered, in preheated 400°F oven 30 to 40 minutes or until squash is tender.

• Spray medium skillet with nonstick cooking spray; heat over medium heat until hot. Add apple, raisins and walnuts; cook over medium heat about 5 minutes or until apples slices are tender.

• For Maple Flavored Syrup, combine apple juice and cornstarch in small saucepan. Cook and stir until thickened and bubbly. Cook and stir 2 minutes more. Remove from heat; stir in butter, Equal®, maple flavoring and vanilla.

• Add Maple Flavored Syrup to apple mixture; cook until heated through, 2 to 3 minutes.

• Place squash wedges on serving platter; spoon apple mixture over squash.

Makes 4 servings

Herbed Green Bean Casserole

¾ cup dried breadcrumbs, divided
2 teaspoons dried basil
½ teaspoon salt
½ teaspoon black pepper
½ teaspoon dried thyme
1 teaspoon dried oregano
2 teaspoons parsley
1 teaspoon garlic powder
1 cup freshly grated Parmesan cheese
½ cup CRISCO® Oil
2 (14-ounce) cans green beans, drained

Preheat oven to 350°F.

Combine first 9 ingredients in a large bowl. Toss well. Add CRISCO® Oil to breadcrumb mixture; stir well. Reserve 2 tablespoons breadcrumb mixture for top of casserole. Combine green beans and breadcrumb mixture in an ovenproof dish and sprinkle with the reserved crumb mixture.

Bake for about 30 minutes or until the top is golden and crispy.

Makes 8 servings

Note: You can replace the canned beans with frozen or blanched and cooled fresh beans. The dried breadcrumbs and herbs can be replaced with Italian-style breadcrumbs.

Orange-Spice Glazed Carrots

  1 package (32 ounces) baby carrots
½ cup packed light brown sugar
½ cup orange juice
  3 tablespoons butter or margarine
¾ teaspoon ground cinnamon
¼ teaspoon ground nutmeg
  2 tablespoons cornstarch
¼ cup cold water

Slow Cooker Directions
Combine all ingredients except cornstarch and water in slow cooker. Cover and cook on LOW 3½ to 4 hours or until carrots are crisp-tender. Spoon carrots into serving bowl. Remove juices to small saucepan. Heat to a boil. Mix cornstarch and water in small bowl until blended. Stir into saucepan. Boil 1 minute or until thickened, stirring constantly. Spoon over carrots.   *Makes 6 servings*

Garlic Greens

5 to 6 ounces fresh spinach leaves
1 tablespoon reduced-fat margarine or olive oil
4 cloves garlic, minced

1. Wash spinach; remove and discard stems. Melt margarine in small skillet over medium heat. Add garlic; cook and stir about 1 minute. Do not allow garlic to brown.

2. Add spinach to skillet; stir to coat with garlic. Cover; cook 1 minute or until spinach is wilted. Serve immediately.   *Makes 2 servings*

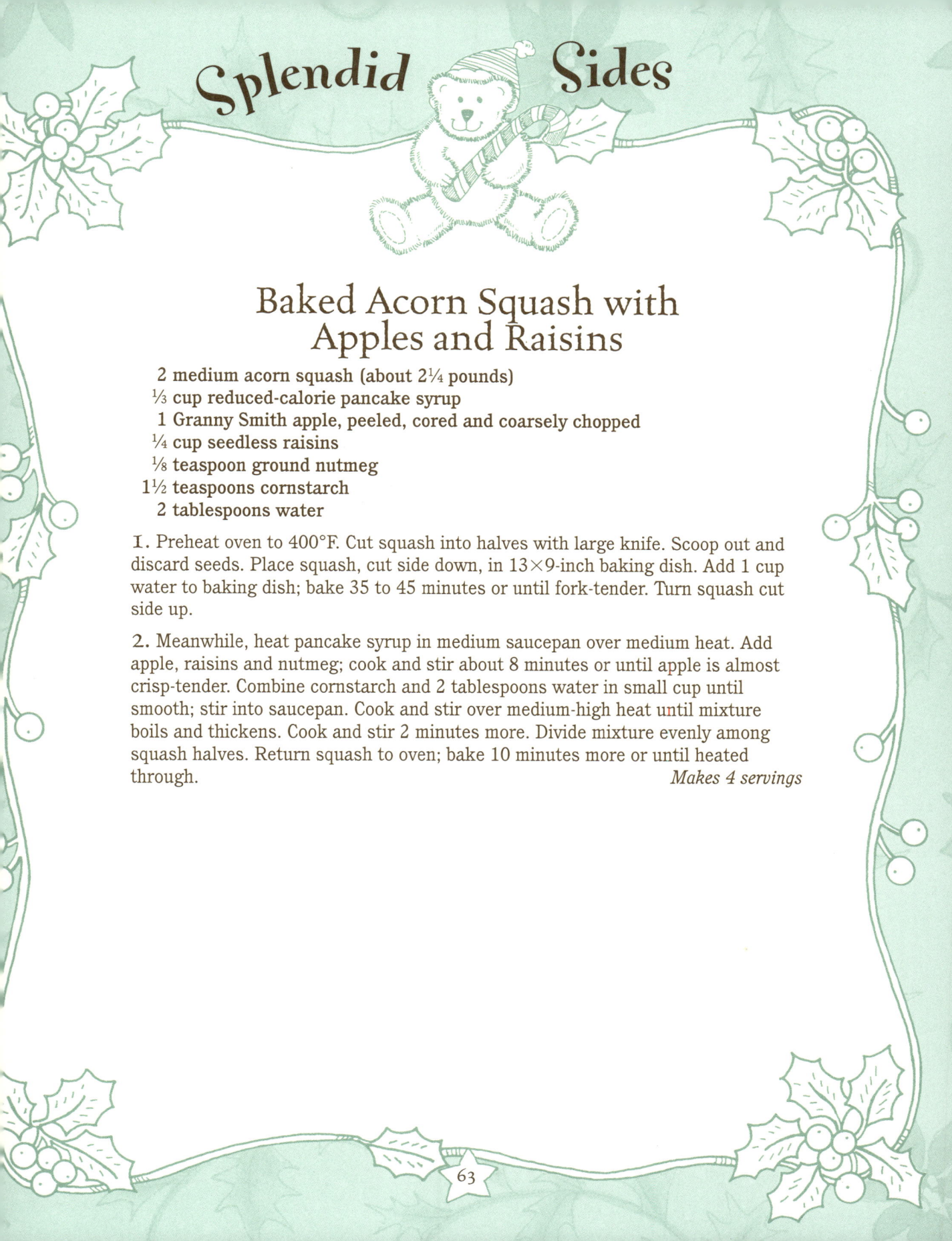

Baked Acorn Squash with Apples and Raisins

    2 medium acorn squash (about 2¼ pounds)
⅓ cup reduced-calorie pancake syrup
    1 Granny Smith apple, peeled, cored and coarsely chopped
¼ cup seedless raisins
⅛ teaspoon ground nutmeg
1½ teaspoons cornstarch
    2 tablespoons water

I. Preheat oven to 400°F. Cut squash into halves with large knife. Scoop out and discard seeds. Place squash, cut side down, in 13×9-inch baking dish. Add 1 cup water to baking dish; bake 35 to 45 minutes or until fork-tender. Turn squash cut side up.

2. Meanwhile, heat pancake syrup in medium saucepan over medium heat. Add apple, raisins and nutmeg; cook and stir about 8 minutes or until apple is almost crisp-tender. Combine cornstarch and 2 tablespoons water in small cup until smooth; stir into saucepan. Cook and stir over medium-high heat until mixture boils and thickens. Cook and stir 2 minutes more. Divide mixture evenly among squash halves. Return squash to oven; bake 10 minutes more or until heated through.

Makes 4 servings

Roasted Butternut Squash

Nonstick cooking spray
1 pound butternut squash, peeled and cut into 1-inch cubes (about 4 cups)
2 medium onions, coarsely chopped
8 ounces carrots, peeled and cut into ½-inch diagonal slices (about 2 cups)
1 tablespoon dark brown sugar
¼ teaspoon salt
Black pepper
1 tablespoon butter or margarine, melted

1. Preheat oven to 400°F. Line large baking sheet with foil and coat with nonstick cooking spray. Arrange vegetables in single layer on foil; coat lightly with cooking spray. Sprinkle vegetables with brown sugar, salt and pepper.

2. Bake 30 minutes. Stir gently; bake 10 to 15 minutes longer or until vegetables are tender. Remove from oven; drizzle with butter and toss to coat.

Makes 5 servings

Spinach Casserole

3 tablespoons butter
1 tablespoon all-purpose flour
1 cup milk
2 eggs, separated
1 tablespoon chopped fresh parsley
  Salt
  Black pepper
1 cup (4 ounces) shredded Cheddar cheese
2 packages (14 ounces each) frozen chopped spinach, thawed and
    squeezed dry

1. Preheat oven to 350°F. Grease 2½-quart casserole.

2. Melt butter in medium saucepan over medium heat. Add flour; cook and stir 2 minutes. Gradually whisk in milk. Continue cooking until mixture thickens slightly. Beat egg yolks. Gradually stir yolks into milk mixture. Season with parsley, salt and pepper. Add cheese, stirring constantly until cheese melts. Transfer to medium bowl.

3. Add spinach to cheese sauce and stir until well combined; keep warm.

4. Beat egg whites in clean, dry bowl at high speed of electric mixer until stiff peaks form. Gently fold egg whites into spinach mixture.

5. Spoon into prepared casserole and bake 40 minutes or until center is set and looks dry. *Do not overbake.*   *Makes 6 servings*

Merry Main Dishes

Glazed Pork Tenderloin

2 whole well-trimmed pork tenderloins (about 1½ pounds total)
½ cup currant jelly or canned jellied cranberry sauce
1 tablespoon bottled grated horseradish
½ cup chicken broth
¼ cup Rhine or other sweet white wine
   Salt and pepper (optional)

1. Preheat oven to 325°F. Place tenderloins on meat rack in shallow roasting pan. Combine jelly and horseradish in microwavable dish or small saucepan. Microwave at HIGH 1 minute or heat over low heat until jelly is melted; stir well. Brush half of mixture over tenderloins. Roast 30 minutes; turn tenderloins over. Brush with remaining jelly mixture. Continue to roast 30 to 40 minutes depending on thickness of tenderloins or until thermometer registers 160°F.*

2. Transfer tenderloins to cutting board; tent with foil. Let stand 10 minutes. Remove meat rack from roasting pan. Pour broth and wine into pan. Place over burners; cook over medium-high heat, stirring frequently and scraping up any browned bits, 4 to 5 minutes or until sauce is reduced to ½ cup. Strain sauce; season to taste with salt and pepper. Carve tenderloins into thin slices. Serve with sauce.

Makes 6 servings

The most accurate way to measure the internal temperature of pork tenderloin is with an instant-read thermometer. Do not leave the thermometer in the tenderloin during roasting since it is not ovenproof.

Merry Main Dishes

Baked Holiday Ham with Cranberry-Wine Compote

2 teaspoons peanut oil
⅔ cup chopped onion
½ cup chopped celery
1 cup red wine
1 cup honey
½ cup sugar
1 package (12 ounces) fresh cranberries
1 fully-cooked smoked ham (10 pounds)
Whole cloves

1. For Cranberry-Wine Compote, heat oil in large saucepan over medium-high heat until hot; add onion and celery. Cook until tender, stirring frequently. Stir in wine, honey and sugar; bring to a boil. Add cranberries; return to a boil. Reduce heat to low; cover and simmer 10 minutes. Cool completely.

2. Carefully ladle enough clear syrup from cranberry mixture into glass measuring cup to equal 1 cup; set aside. Transfer remaining cranberry mixture to small serving bowl; cover and refrigerate.

3. Slice away skin from ham with sharp utility knife. (Omit step if meat retailer has already removed skin.)

4. Preheat oven to 325°F. Score fat on ham in diamond design with sharp utility knife; stud with whole cloves. Place ham, fat side up, on rack in shallow roasting pan.

5. Bake, uncovered, 1½ hours. Baste ham with reserved cranberry-wine syrup. Bake 1 to 2 hours more or until meat thermometer inserted into thickest part of ham, not touching bone, registers 140°F, basting with cranberry-wine syrup twice.*

6. Let ham stand 10 minutes before transferring to warm serving platter. Cut ham into large slices. Serve warm with chilled Cranberry-Wine Compote.

Makes 16 to 20 servings

*Total cooking time for ham should be 18 to 24 minutes per pound.

Veal Chops with Brandied Apricots and Pecans

    ¼ cup water
    ¼ cup honey
     8 dried apricot halves, cut into ¼-inch slices
     4 (¾-inch-thick) boneless veal chops (about 5 ounces each)*
    ¼ teaspoon salt
    ¼ teaspoon black pepper
     3 tablespoons all-purpose flour
     2 tablespoons butter or margarine
    16 pecan halves
     2 tablespoons brandy

If boneless chops are unavailable, chops with bones can be substituted.

1. Combine water and honey in 2-cup glass measuring cup; microwave at HIGH 2 minutes or until mixture begins to boil. Stir in apricots; cover with plastic wrap, turning back 1 corner to vent. Microwave 30 seconds. Cover; let stand 1 hour.

2. Meanwhile, sprinkle veal chops with salt and pepper. Place flour in shallow bowl; dredge 1 veal chop at a time in flour, shaking off excess.

3. Melt butter in large skillet over medium heat; arrange veal chops and pecan halves in single layer in skillet. Cook veal chops and pecans 5 minutes per side or until browned.

4. Add apricot mixture and brandy; bring to a boil. Reduce heat to low; cover and simmer 10 minutes or until veal chops are tender.

5. Remove veal chops and pecans from skillet. Bring apricot mixture in skillet to a boil over high heat; cook 1 minute or until slightly thickened. Spoon apricot mixture over veal chops.   *Makes 4 servings*

Roasted Herb & Garlic Tenderloin

1 beef tenderloin roast, trimmed (3 to 4 pounds)
1 tablespoon black peppercorns
2 tablespoons chopped fresh basil *or* 2 teaspoons dried basil leaves
4½ teaspoons chopped fresh thyme *or* 1½ teaspoons dried thyme leaves
1 tablespoon chopped fresh rosemary *or* 1 teaspoon dried rosemary
1 tablespoon minced garlic
Salt and black pepper (optional)

1. Preheat oven to 425°F. Tie roast with cotton string at 1½-inch intervals to hold shape of roast. Place roast on meat rack in shallow roasting pan.

2. Place peppercorns in small heavy resealable plastic food storage bag. Squeeze out excess air; seal bag tightly. Pound peppercorns with flat side of meat mallet or rolling pin until peppercorns are cracked.

3. Combine cracked peppercorns, basil, thyme, rosemary and garlic in small bowl; rub over top surface of roast.

4. Roast 40 to 50 minutes until internal temperature reaches 135°F for medium-rare or 150°F for medium when tested with meat thermometer inserted into the thickest part of roast.

5. Transfer roast to cutting board; cover with foil. Let stand 10 to 15 minutes before carving. Internal temperature will continue to rise 5°F to 10°F during stand time. Remove and discard string. To serve, carve crosswise into ½-inch-thick slices. Season with salt and pepper, if desired. *Makes 10 to 12 servings*

Chicken with Orange Almond Sauce

Butter-flavored cooking spray
4 (4-ounce) skinless boneless chicken breast halves
1 cup orange juice
⅓ cup SPLENDA® Granular
2 tablespoons cornstarch
1 can (11 ounces) mandarin oranges, rinsed and drained
2 tablespoons slivered almonds
1 teaspoon dried onion flakes
1 teaspoon dried parsley flakes

1. In large skillet sprayed with cooking spray, brown chicken pieces for 4 to 5 minutes on each side.

2. Meanwhile, in covered jar, combine orange juice, SPLENDA®, and cornstarch. Shake well to blend.

3. Pour sauce mixture into medium saucepan sprayed with cooking spray. Cook over medium heat until mixture thickens, stirring constantly. Remove from heat.

4. Stir mandarin oranges, almonds, onion flakes, and parsley flakes into sauce. Spoon sauce evenly over browned chicken pieces.

5. Reduce heat and simmer for 5 minutes. When serving, evenly spoon sauce over chicken pieces.
Makes 4 servings

Pork Roast with Dried Cranberries and Apricots

  1 center cut pork loin roast (3½ pounds)
1½ cups cranberry-apple juice, divided
  1 cup chardonnay or other dry white wine
1½ teaspoons ground ginger
  1 teaspoon ground cardamom
  2 tablespoons apricot preserves
¼ cup water
  1 tablespoon plus 1 teaspoon cornstarch
½ cup dried cranberries
½ cup chopped dried apricots
  2 tablespoons golden raisins

1. Place pork roast in large resealable plastic food storage bag. Combine 1 cup cranberry-apple juice, chardonnay, ginger and cardamom in medium bowl. Pour over roast, turning to coat. Seal bag. Marinate in refrigerator 4 hours or overnight, turning several times.

2. Preheat oven to 350°F. Remove roast from marinade; reserve marinade. Place roast in roasting pan. Pour marinade over roast. Bake, loosely covered with foil, 1 hour. Remove foil and continue baking 30 minutes or until internal temperature reaches 165°F when tested with a meat thermometer inserted into the thickest part of roast not touching bone. Transfer roast to cutting board; cover with foil. Internal temperature will continue to rise 5°F to 10°F during stand time.

3. Measure juices from pan. Add enough remaining cranberry-apple juice to equal 1½ cups. Combine juices and apricot preserves in small saucepan. Stir water into cornstarch in cup until smooth; stir into juice mixture. Bring to a boil over medium heat. Cook until thickened, stirring frequently. Add dried cranberries, apricots and raisins. Cook 2 minutes; remove from heat. Cut roast into thin slices. Drizzle some sauce over roast; serve with remaining sauce. Garnish, if desired.

Makes 10 servings

Ham with Cherry Sauce

5 pound fully cooked boneless ham
   Whole cloves

Cherry Sauce
   2 cans (16 ounces each) red tart pitted cherries in juice, undrained (see Tip)
   ⅔ to ¾ cup unsweetened pineapple juice
   4 teaspoons lemon juice
   ¼ cup cornstarch
   1 to 1½ cups EQUAL® SPOONFUL*
   Red food coloring (optional)
   Parsley sprigs

May substitute 24 packets Equal® sweetener.

• Place ham in roasting pan; stud with cloves. Roast ham in preheated 325°F oven about 1½ hours or until thermometer inserted in center of ham registers 160°F.

• For Cherry Sauce, drain cherries, reserving juice in 2-cup glass measure. Add enough pineapple juice to make 2 cups. Pour juice mixture and lemon juice into medium saucepan; whisk in cornstarch until smooth.

• Heat to a boil, whisking constantly, about 1 minute. Add cherries to saucepan; cook over medium heat 3 to 4 minutes or until heated through. Stir in Equal® and food coloring, if desired. (Makes about 4⅔ cups sauce.)

• Slice ham and arrange on platter with bowl of Cherry Sauce in center. Garnish with parsley.   *Makes 16 servings*

Tip: 2 packages (16 ounces each) frozen no-sugar-added pitted cherries, thawed, can be substituted for the canned cherries; drain cherries thoroughly and add enough pineapple juice to make 2 cups. Proceed with recipe as directed above.

Oven Roasted Chicken

1 whole chicken (about 4 to 4½ pounds)
2 tablespoons olive oil
1 tablespoon LAWRY'S® Seasoned Salt
1 teaspoon LAWRY'S® Seasoned Pepper

Rinse chicken and pat dry. Rub olive oil over entire surface of chicken. Generously sprinkle Seasoned Salt and Seasoned Pepper over outside and inside cavity of chicken. Spray 13×9×2-inch baking dish and roasting rack with nonstick cooking spray. Place chicken breast-side-up on roasting rack. Roast in 400°F oven until chicken is no longer pink and juices run clear when cut (175° to 180°F at thickest joint), about 60 to 70 minutes. Let stand 10 minutes before carving.

Makes 8 servings

Hint: Loosely 'crunch up' some foil in dish around chicken to keep grease from splattering in oven.

Prep. Time: 10 minutes
Cook Time: 60 to 70 minutes

Cranberry-Onion Pork Roast

1 boneless pork loin roast (about 2 pounds)
1 can (16 ounces) whole cranberry sauce
1 package (1 ounce) dried onion soup mix

Season roast with salt and pepper; place over indirect heat on grill; stir together cranberry sauce and onion soup mix and heat, covered, in microwave until hot, about one minute. Baste roast with cranberry mixture every 10 minutes until roast is done (internal temperature with a meat thermometer is 155° to 160°F), about 30 to 45 minutes. Let roast rest about 5 to 8 minutes before slicing to serve. Heat any leftover basting mixture to boiling, stir and boil for 5 minutes and serve alongside roast.

Makes 4 to 6 servings

*Favorite recipe from **National Pork Board***

Herb-Roasted Racks of Lamb

½ cup mango chutney, chopped
2 to 3 cloves garlic, minced
2 whole racks (6 ribs each) lamb loin chops (2½ to 3 pounds)
1 cup fresh French or Italian bread crumbs
1 tablespoon chopped fresh thyme *or* 1 teaspoon dried thyme leaves
1 tablespoon chopped fresh rosemary *or* 1 teaspoon dried rosemary
1 tablespoon chopped fresh oregano *or* 1 teaspoon dried oregano leaves

1. Preheat oven to 400°F. Combine chutney and garlic in small bowl; spread evenly over meaty side of lamb with thin spatula. Combine remaining ingredients in separate small bowl; pat crumb mixture evenly over chutney mixture.

2. Place lamb racks, crumb sides up, on rack in shallow roasting pan. Roast in oven 30 to 35 minutes for medium or until internal temperature reaches 145°F when tested with meat thermometer inserted into the thickest part of lamb not touching bone.

3. Place lamb on cutting board; let stand 10 to 15 minutes before carving. Internal temperature will continue to rise 5°F to 10°F during stand time. Slice between ribs into individual chops. Garnish with additional fresh herbs and mango slices, if desired. Serve immediately. *Makes 4 servings*

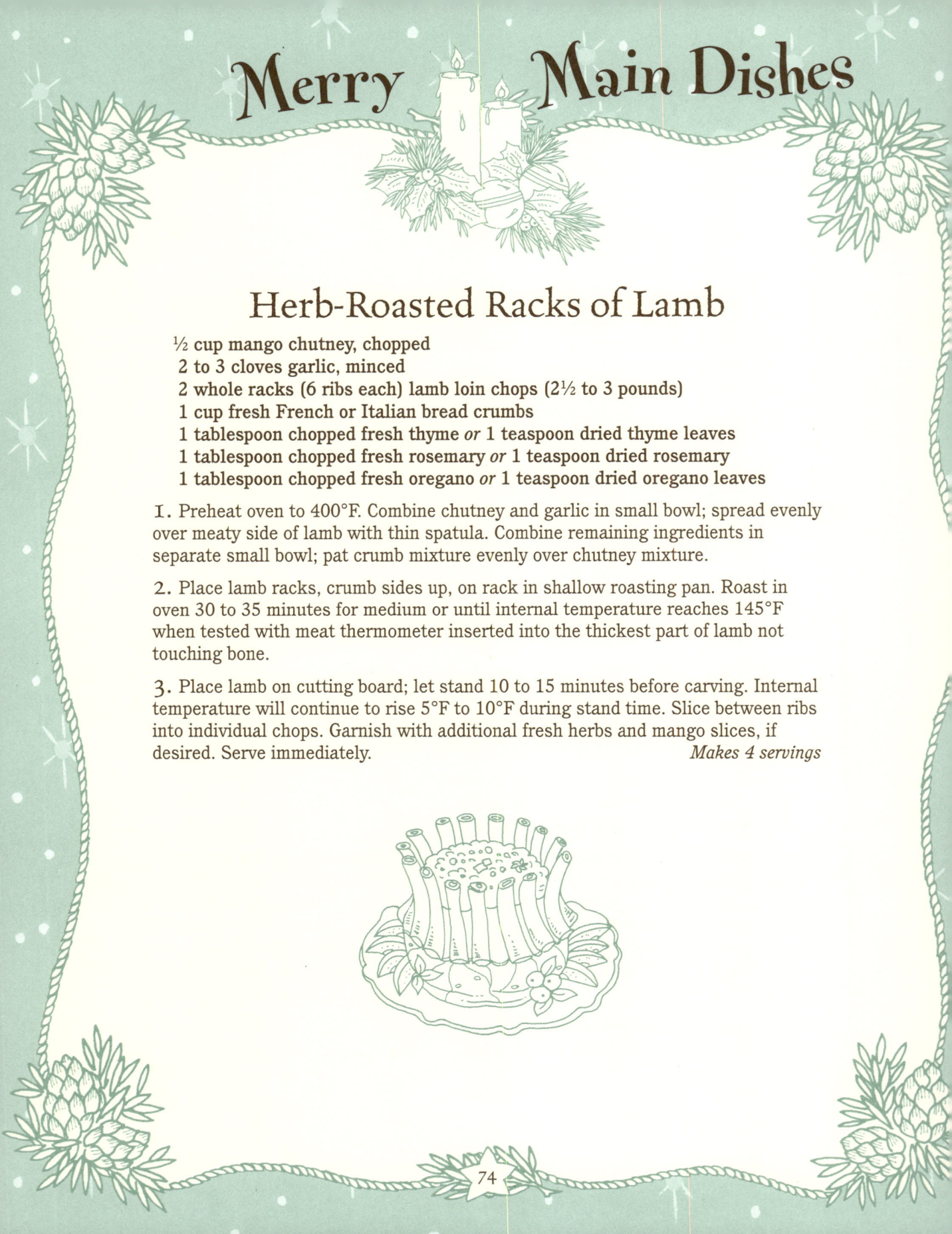

Honey Mustard Pecan Chicken

4 boneless skinless chicken breast halves
¼ cup *French's*® Sweet & Tangy Honey Mustard
1 cup finely chopped pecans

1. Preheat oven to 400°F. Spread mustard evenly on chicken. Coat with pecans pressing gently to adhere.

2. Place chicken in greased and foil-lined baking pan. Bake 20 minutes or until chicken is no longer pink in center. Serve with additional mustard.

Makes 4 servings

Prep Time: 10 minutes
Cook Time: 20 minutes

Maple Cider Basted Turkey

1 PERDUE® Fresh Whole Turkey Breast (4 to 7 pounds)
1 to 2 tablespoons canola oil
1 tablespoon grainy, "country-style" mustard
    Salt and ground pepper to taste
1 apple, cored but unpeeled, sliced thinly
¼ cup maple syrup
2 tablespoons cider vinegar
    Dash Worcestershire sauce

Preheat oven to 350°F. Pat breast dry with paper towel. In small bowl, mix oil and mustard, rub over breast and under skin from neck end. Do not detach skin at base. Season with salt and pepper. Slide apple slices between skin and meat. If necessary, reinsert BIRD-WATCHER® Thermometer to original location. Place breast in roasting pan and roast, uncovered, 1½ to 1¾ hours, until BIRD-WATCHER® Thermometer pops up and meat thermometer inserted in thickest part of breast registers 170°F.

Meanwhile, combine syrup, vinegar and Worcestershire sauce. During last 20 minutes of roasting, baste breast with mixture. If skin is browning too quickly, tent with foil. Remove breast to serving platter and let rest 10 to 15 minutes before carving.

Makes 6 to 8 servings

Marinated Pork Roast

½ cup GRANDMA'S® Molasses
½ cup Dijon mustard
¼ cup tarragon vinegar
    Boneless pork loin roast (3 to 4 pounds)

1. In large plastic bowl, combine molasses, mustard and tarragon vinegar; mix well. Add pork to molasses mixture, turning to coat all sides. Marinate, covered, 1 to 2 hours at room temperature or overnight in refrigerator, turning several times.

2. Heat oven to 325°F. Remove pork from marinade; reserve marinade. Place pork in shallow roasting pan. Cook for 1 to 2 hours or until meat thermometer inserted into thickest part of roast reaches 160°F, basting with marinade* every 30 minutes; discard remaining marinade. *Makes 6 to 8 servings*

*Do not baste during last 5 minutes of cooking.

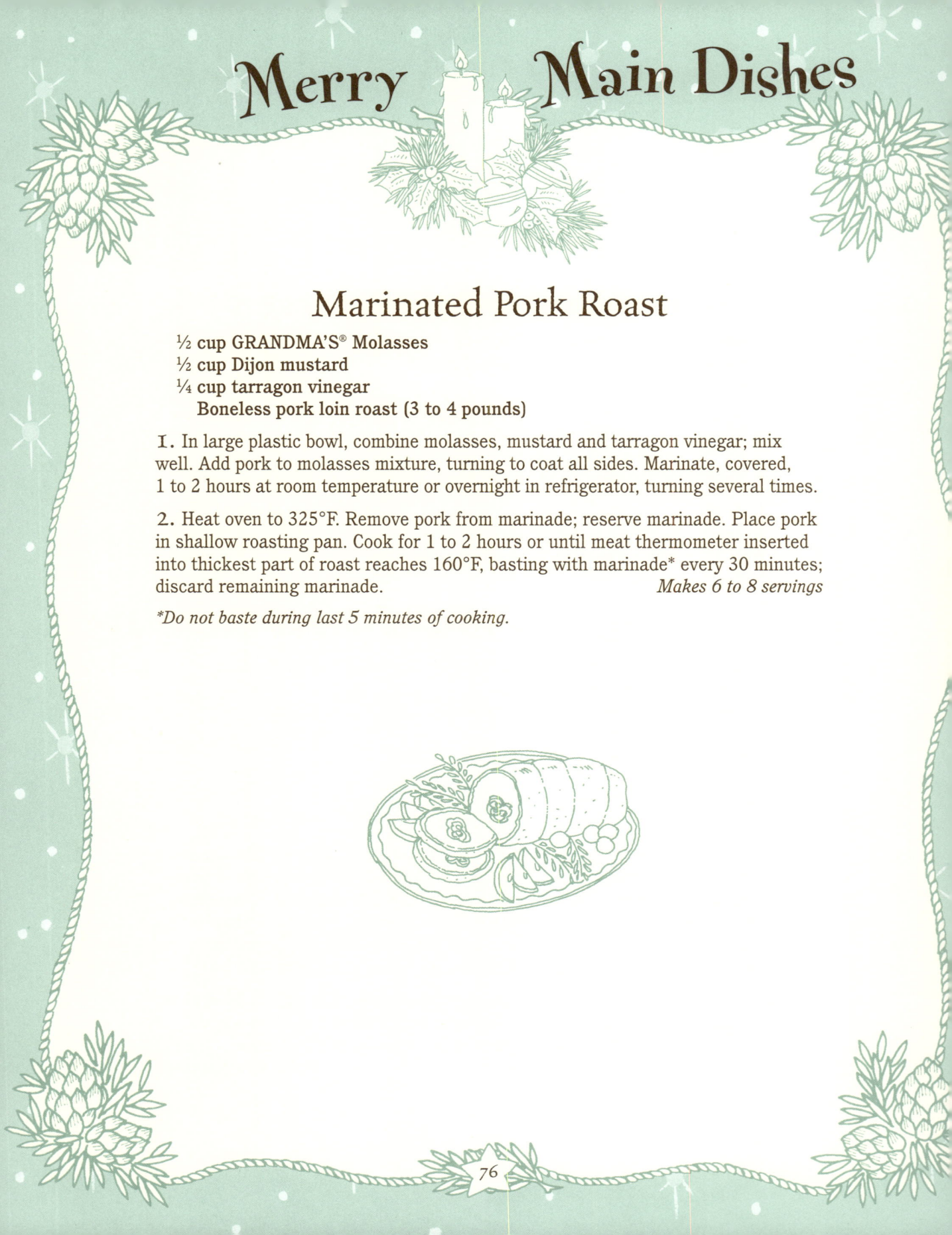

Holiday Baked Ham

1 bone-in smoked ham (8½ pounds)
1 can (20 ounces) DOLE® Pineapple Slices
1 cup apricot preserves
1 teaspoon dry mustard
½ teaspoon ground allspice
   Whole cloves
   Maraschino cherries

● Preheat oven to 325°F. Remove rind from ham. Place ham on rack in open roasting pan, fat side up. Insert meat thermometer with bulb in thickest part away from fat or bone. Roast ham in oven about 3 hours.

● Drain pineapple slices; reserve syrup. In small saucepan, combine syrup, preserves, mustard and allspice. Bring to a boil; continue boiling, stirring occasionally, 10 minutes. Remove ham from oven, but keep oven hot. Stud ham with cloves; brush with glaze. Using wooden picks, secure pineapple slices and cherries to ham. Brush again with glaze. Return ham to oven. Roast 30 minutes longer or until thermometer registers 160°F (about 25 minutes per pound total cooking time). Brush with glaze 15 minutes before done. Let ham stand 20 minutes before slicing.   *Makes 8 to 10 servings*

Citrus Roasted Chicken

1 large foil cooking bag
1 tablespoon all-purpose flour
1 whole chicken (3 to 4 pounds)
½ cup chopped onion
2 tablespoons butter
  Juice of 1 lemon
  Juice of 1 lime
2 teaspoons grated lemon peel
¼ teaspoon salt
½ teaspoon dried thyme leaves
1 tablespoon fresh minced parsley

1. Preheat oven to 450°F. Place foil bag in 1-inch deep baking pan. Spray inside of bag with nonstick cooking spray. Dust with flour.

2. Rinse chicken and pat dry with paper towels. Remove and discard any excess fat. Place onion in chicken cavity and rub skin with butter. Place chicken in foil bag. Squeeze juice of lemon and lime over chicken. Sprinkle with grated lemon peel, salt and thyme. Seal foil bag, leaving head space for heat circulation.

3. Bake 1 hour or until juices run clear and thermometer inserted into thickest part of thigh registers 180°F. Remove from oven. Allow to cool 5 minutes before opening bag. Slit open top of bag to expose chicken; return to oven to brown skin, if desired. Garnish with fresh parsley. *Makes 6 servings*

Quick Tip: For more citrus flavor, add thinly sliced rounds of lemon and lime to the foil bag. The fruit will add more aroma as it cooks with the chicken.

Orange-Glazed Chicken

  1 teaspoon salt
½ teaspoon black pepper
  1 broiler-fryer chicken (2½ to 3 pounds), cut in half
½ cup orange marmalade
  3 tablespoons butter
  1 tablespoon dried onion flakes
  1 clove garlic, minced
¼ teaspoon dried thyme leaves
    Orange wedges, for garnish
    Parsley or cilantro, for garnish

1. Combine salt and pepper; rub over chicken. Arrange chicken, breast side up, in 13×9-inch baking pan. Bake, uncovered, 30 minutes.

2. Combine marmalade, butter, onion, garlic and thyme in medium saucepan. Heat 1 to 2 minutes, stirring frequently. Baste chicken with marmalade mixture 2 to 3 times.

3. Bake, uncovered, 15 to 20 minutes or until chicken is no longer pink in center and juices run clear. Remove from oven. Discard remaining marmalade mixture. Garnish with orange wedges and parsley or cilantro. *Makes 4 to 6 servings*

Beef Burgundy

2½ pounds boneless beef round steak
4 cloves garlic, chopped
½ cup chopped onion
2 cups dry red wine
1 (10¾-ounce) can condensed cream of mushroom soup, undiluted
1½ cups dried tart cherries
2 (4½-ounce) jars button mushrooms, drained
3 tablespoons all-purpose flour
½ cup water
Egg noodles or bow-tie pasta, cooked and well drained

Trim fat from steak; cut steak into 1-inch cubes. Coat a large, oven-proof Dutch oven or stockpot with non-stick cooking spray; place over medium heat until hot. Add steak; cook, stirring occasionally, 8 to 10 minutes, or until meat is brown. Drain well; set aside.

Recoat pan with cooking spray; place over medium heat. Add garlic and onion; sauté 1 minute. Add wine and mushroom soup; mix well. Bring mixture to a boil. Return steak to pan; stir in cherries and mushrooms.

Combine flour and water in a small bowl; blend until smooth with a fork or wire whisk. Gradually stir flour mixture into steak mixture; mix well. Bake, covered, in a preheated 350°F oven 1½ hours, or until steak is tender and mixture is thick. Serve over cooked noodles or pasta. *Makes 8 servings*

Favorite recipe from **Cherry Marketing Institute**

Pork Chops with Glazed Apples

1 tablespoon vegetable oil
4 boneless pork chops, ¼ inch thick
½ teaspoon ground sage
  Salt
  Black pepper
2 large Granny Smith apples, thinly sliced
2 tablespoons sugar
½ teaspoon ground cinnamon

1. Heat oil in large skillet over medium heat. Add pork chops; sprinkle with sage.

2. Cook 8 minutes or until no longer pink in center, turning after 4 minutes. Season with salt and pepper to taste. Remove pork chops from skillet; keep warm.

3. Add apples, sugar and cinnamon to skillet. Reduce heat to low; cover. Cook 5 minutes, stirring occasionally. Serve over pork chops.   *Makes 4 servings*

Herbed Turkey Breast with Orange Sauce

1 large onion, chopped
3 cloves garlic, minced
1 teaspoon dried rosemary
½ teaspoon black pepper
1 boneless skinless turkey breast (2 to 3 pounds)
1½ cups orange juice

Slow Cooker Directions

1. Place onion in slow cooker. Combine garlic, rosemary and pepper in small bowl; set aside. Cut slices about three fourths of the way through turkey at 2-inch intervals. Rub garlic mixture between slices.

2. Place turkey, cut side up, in slow cooker. Pour orange juice over turkey. Cover; cook on LOW 7 to 8 hours or until internal temperature reaches 170°F when tested with meat thermometer inserted into the thickest part of breast.

3. Transfer turkey to cutting board; cover with foil and let stand 10 to 15 minutes before carving. Internal temperature will rise 5°F to 10°F during stand time. Serve sauce from slow cooker with sliced turkey.   *Makes 4 to 6 servings*

Almond Crusted Chicken Breasts

1½ cups BLUE DIAMOND® Sliced Natural Almonds, lightly toasted
2 whole chicken breasts, skinned, boned and cut in half
  Salt
  Pepper
¼ cup flour
1 egg, beaten with 2 teaspoons water
¼ cup butter, melted
1 teaspoon lemon juice
1½ teaspoons chopped fresh basil or ½ teaspoon dried basil

With hands, lightly crush almonds into small pieces; reserve. Lightly flatten chicken breasts. Season with salt and pepper. Dredge chicken in flour. Pat off excess flour. Dip chicken in beaten egg. Press each chicken breast in almonds, covering chicken well. Place on buttered baking sheet. Bake at 425°F. for 10 to 15 minutes or until chicken is just firm and no longer pink in center, and almonds are golden. Meanwhile, combine butter, lemon juice and basil. Drizzle over cooked chicken breasts.

Makes 4 servings

Zesty Chicken & Rice Supper

2 boneless skinless chicken breasts, cut into 1-inch pieces
2 large bell peppers, coarsely chopped
1 can (28 ounces) diced tomatoes, undrained
1 cup uncooked white rice
1 cup water
1 small onion, chopped
1 package (about 1 ounce) taco seasoning
1 teaspoon salt
1 teaspoon black pepper
1 teaspoon ground red pepper
    Shredded Cheddar cheese (optional)

Slow Cooker Directions
Combine all ingredients, except cheese, in slow cooker; mix well. Cover; cook on
LOW 6 to 8 hours or on HIGH 3 to 4 hours. Garnish with cheese, if desired.

Makes 3 to 4 servings

Turkey with Herb Dressing

16 cups (½-inch thick) bread cubes
⅓ cup dried parsley flakes
2 teaspoons salt
2 teaspoons crushed rosemary
2 teaspoons ground thyme
1 teaspoon ground sage
½ CRISCO® Stick or ½ cup CRISCO® Shortening
1 cup coarsely chopped onion
1 cup coarsely chopped celery
1½ cups chicken broth
1 turkey (14 to 15 pounds)
Butter Flavor CRISCO® Shortening, melted, for basting

Preheat oven to 325°F.

Combine bread cubes, parsley, salt, rosemary, thyme and sage in a large bowl. Toss to mix.

Melt CRISCO® Shortening in a skillet over medium heat. Mix in onion and celery; cook for 3 minutes, stirring occasionally. Toss with the bread mixture. Add chicken broth, mixing gently until ingredients are thoroughly blended.

Rinse turkey with cold water; pat dry, inside and out, with paper towels. Fill body and neck cavities with the stuffing. Fasten neck skin to back with a skewer. Bring wing tips onto back of bird. Push drumsticks under band of skin at tail, if present, or tie to tail with cord.

Place turkey breast-side-up on a rack in a shallow roasting pan. Insert meat thermometer in the thickest part of the inner thigh muscle; be sure tip does not touch bone.

Roast for 4 to 5 hours or until thermometer registers 180°F to 185°F; baste frequently with CRISCO® Shortening during roasting.

Remove stuffing immediately from bird. For easier carving, let stand 15 to 20 minutes after removing from oven.   *Makes 10 to 14 servings*

Herbed Chicken and Potatoes

2 medium all-purpose potatoes, thinly sliced (about 1 pound)
4 bone-in chicken breast halves (about 2 pounds)*
1 envelope LIPTON® RECIPE SECRETS® Savory Herb with Garlic Soup Mix
⅓ cup water
1 tablespoon BERTOLLI® Olive Oil

Substitution: Use 1 (2½- to 3-pound) chicken, cut into serving pieces.

1. Preheat oven to 425°F. In 13×9-inch baking or roasting pan, add potatoes; arrange chicken over potatoes.

2. Pour soup mix blended with water and oil over chicken and potatoes.

3. Bake uncovered 40 minutes or until chicken is thoroughly cooked and potatoes are tender. *Makes 4 servings*

Rack of Lamb with Dijon-Mustard Sauce

1 rack of lamb (3 pounds), all visible fat removed
1 cup finely chopped fresh parsley
½ cup Dijon mustard
½ cup soft whole wheat bread crumbs
1 tablespoon chopped fresh rosemary *or* 2 teaspoons dried rosemary
1 teaspoon minced garlic
Fresh rosemary, lemon slices and lemon peel strips (optional)

Preheat oven to 500°F. Place lamb in large baking pan. Combine parsley, mustard, bread crumbs, rosemary and garlic in small bowl. Spread evenly over top of lamb. Place in center of oven; cook 7 minutes for medium-rare. Turn off oven but do not open door for 30 minutes. Garnish with additional fresh rosemary, lemon slices and lemon peel strips, if desired. *Makes 6 servings*

Merry Main Dishes

Apple Stuffed Pork Loin Roast

2 cloves garlic, minced
1 teaspoon coarse salt
1 teaspoon dried rosemary
½ teaspoon dried thyme leaves
½ teaspoon freshly ground black pepper
1 boneless center cut pork loin roast (4 to 5 pounds), tied
1 tablespoon butter
2 large tart apples, peeled, cored and thinly sliced (2 cups)
1 medium onion, cut into thin strips (about 1 cup)
2 tablespoons brown sugar
1 teaspoon Dijon mustard
1 cup apple cider or apple juice

1. Preheat oven to 325°F. Combine garlic, salt, rosemary, thyme and pepper in small bowl. Untie pork roast. If roast is not precut, cut lengthwise down roast almost to, but not through the bottom. Open like a book. Rub half garlic mixture onto cut sides of pork.

2. Melt butter in large skillet over medium-high heat. Add onion and apples; sauté 5 to 10 minutes or until soft. Stir in brown sugar and mustard. Spread mixture evenly on one cut side of roast. Close halves; tie roast with cotton string at 2-inch intervals. Place roast on meat rack in shallow roasting pan. Pour apple juice over roast. Rub outside of roast with remaining garlic mixture.

3. Roast, uncovered, basting frequently with pan drippings, 2 to 2½ hours or until an instant-read thermometer inserted in thickest part registers 155°F. Let roast stand for 15 minutes before slicing. Internal temperature will continue to rise 5°F to 10°F during stand time. Carve roast crosswise. *Makes 16 servings*

Cherry-Glazed Chicken

1 (2½- to 3-pound) broiler-fryer chicken, cut up
   (or 6 chicken breast halves, skinned and boned)
½ cup milk
½ cup all-purpose flour
1 teaspoon dried thyme
   Salt and pepper, to taste
1 to 2 tablespoons vegetable oil
1 (16-ounce) can unsweetened tart cherries
¼ cup brown sugar
¼ cup granulated sugar
1 teaspoon prepared yellow mustard

Rinse chicken; pat dry with paper towels. Pour milk into a shallow container. In another container, combine flour, thyme, salt and pepper. Dip chicken first in milk, then in flour mixture; coat evenly. Heat oil in a large skillet. Add chicken; brown on all sides. Place chicken in 13×9×2-inch baking dish. Bake, covered with aluminum foil, in preheated 350°F oven 30 minutes.

Meanwhile, drain cherries, reserving ½ cup juice. Combine cherry juice, brown sugar and granulated sugar in small saucepan; mix well. Bring mixture to a boil over medium heat. Add mustard; mix well. Cook 5 minutes, or until sauce is syrupy. Stir in cherries.

After chicken has cooked 30 minutes, remove baking dish from oven and carefully remove foil cover. Spoon hot cherry mixture evenly over chicken. Bake, uncovered, 15 minutes, or until chicken is no longer pink in center. Serve immediately.

Makes 6 servings

Favorite recipe from **Cherry Marketing Institute**

Pork Tenderloin with Thyme and White Beans

2 to 3 pork tenderloins (2 to 3 pounds) *or* 1 boneless pork top
    loin roast (3 to 4 pounds)
1 bulb garlic, peeled and separated into cloves
  Salt
  White pepper
2 cups navy beans, soaked overnight
1 cup red wine
¾ cup white wine
¼ cup hot water
2 tablespoons dried thyme leaves
2 teaspoons dried oregano leaves
1 teaspoon chopped garlic
1 teaspoon baking soda
2 yellow onions, quartered
1 medium leek, cut into ⅛-inch-thick slices
1 tablespoon olive oil
1 tablespoon unsalted butter, melted

Slow Cooker Directions

1. With a paring knife, poke holes about 1 inch deep evenly around tenderloins. Place one peeled clove into each hole. Season to taste with salt and white pepper.

2. Drain beans; place into slow cooker. Add wines, water, thyme, oregano, garlic and baking soda; mix well. Top with onions, leek and pork. Combine oil and butter and pour over pork.

3. Cover; cook on LOW 6 to 8 hours or until beans are tender and pork is cooked through.
Makes 10 to 12 servings

Cranberry Smothered Chicken

½ cup all-purpose flour
  Salt and white pepper
3 whole chicken breasts, split and skinned
¼ cup vegetable oil
3 cloves garlic, minced
½ cup chicken broth
2 tablespoons butter or margarine
3 medium onions, coarsely chopped
2 medium green bell peppers, cut into thin strips
10 large mushrooms, sliced
½ cup raspberry or balsamic vinegar
1 can (16 ounces) whole berry cranberry sauce
1 cup orange juice
1 tablespoon cornstarch
1 tablespoon Worcestershire sauce
  Hot cooked rice (optional)

1. Combine flour, salt and white pepper in large resealable plastic food storage bag. Add chicken to bag; shake to coat completely with flour mixture.

2. Heat oil in large skillet over medium-high heat. Add garlic; cook until soft. Add chicken; cook until chicken is browned on both sides. Drain drippings from skillet. Add chicken broth; bring to a boil over high heat. Reduce heat to low. Cover; simmer 30 minutes.

3. Melt butter in another large skillet over medium-high heat. Cook and stir onions, bell peppers and mushrooms in hot butter until vegetables are softened. Stir in vinegar, cranberry sauce and orange juice. Reduce heat to medium. Cook and stir about 5 minutes or until cranberry sauce melts and mixture is heated through.

4. Combine cornstarch and Worcestershire sauce with enough water to make a smooth paste; add to sauce and vegetables in skillet. Stir gently over low heat until thickened. Season with salt and white pepper.

5. Serve chicken with sauce and rice, if desired. *Makes 6 servings*

Cranberry-Glazed Cornish Hens with Wild Rice

1 box UNCLE BEN'S® Long Grain & Wild Rice Fast Cook Recipe
½ cup sliced celery
⅓ cup slivered almonds (optional)
1 can (8 ounces) jellied cranberry sauce, divided
4 Cornish hens, thawed (about 1 pound each)
2 tablespoons olive oil, divided

1. Heat oven to 425°F. Prepare rice according to package directions. Stir in celery, almonds and ½ of cranberry sauce; cool.

2. Spoon about ¾ cup rice mixture into cavity of each hen. Tie drumsticks together with cotton string. Place hens on rack in roasting pan. Brush each hen with some of the oil. Roast 35 to 45 minutes or until juices run clear, basting occasionally with remaining oil.

3. Meanwhile, in small saucepan, heat remaining cranberry sauce until melted. Remove hens from oven; remove and discard string. Spoon cranberry sauce over hens.

Makes 4 servings

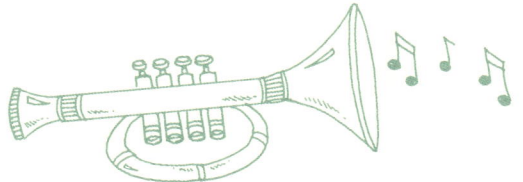

Orange Herbed Chicken and Rice

6 chicken breast halves (about 2¼ pounds)
Vegetable cooking spray
1½ cups orange juice
¼ cup dry white wine
2 teaspoons dried oregano
¾ teaspoon garlic powder
½ teaspoon dried sage
½ teaspoon dried rosemary
½ teaspoon dried thyme
½ teaspoon ground black pepper
Salt to taste (optional)
Paprika
1 tablespoon cornstarch
2 tablespoons cold water
¼ cup orange marmalade
3 cups hot cooked rice
Orange slices for garnish

Place chicken, skin side down, in 13×9-inch glass baking dish coated with cooking spray. Combine orange juice, wine, oregano, garlic powder, sage, rosemary, thyme, pepper and salt in medium bowl. Pour over chicken. Sprinkle with paprika. Cover; bake at 350°F 30 minutes. Turn chicken; sprinkle with paprika. Bake, uncovered, 30 to 40 minutes more or until fork can be inserted into chicken with ease and juices run clear, not pink. Pour pan juices into small saucepan; skim off fat. Combine cornstarch and water in small bowl; add cornstarch mixture and marmalade to saucepan. Cook until sauce is clear and thickened, stirring constantly. Serve chicken and sauce over hot rice. Garnish with orange slices.

Makes 6 servings

Favorite recipe from **USA Rice Federation**

Lamb Chops with Mustard Sauce

1 teaspoon dried thyme leaves
½ teaspoon salt
¼ teaspoon black pepper
4 center cut loin lamb chops (about 1½ pounds total), cut 1½ inches thick
2 tablespoons canola or vegetable oil
¼ cup finely chopped shallots or sweet onion
¼ cup beef or chicken broth
2 tablespoons Worcestershire sauce
1½ tablespoons Dijon mustard
Chopped fresh thyme (optional)

1. Sprinkle thyme, salt and pepper over lamb. Heat oil in large skillet over medium heat. Add chops; cook 4 minutes per side. Transfer chops to a plate; set aside.

2. Add shallots to skillet; cook 3 minutes, stirring occasionally. Lower heat to medium-low. Add broth, Worcestershire sauce and mustard; simmer 5 minutes or until sauce thickens slightly, stirring occasionally. Return chops to skillet; cook 2 minutes for medium-rare, turning once. Transfer to serving plates; top with fresh thyme, if desired.   *Makes 4 servings*

Turkey Breast with Barley-Cranberry Stuffing

2 cups fat-free reduced-sodium chicken broth
1 cup uncooked quick-cooking barley
½ cup chopped onion
½ cup dried cranberries
2 tablespoons slivered almonds, toasted
½ teaspoon rubbed sage
½ teaspoon garlic-pepper seasoning
  Nonstick cooking spray
1 fresh or frozen bone-in turkey breast half (about 2 pounds),
  thawed and skinned
⅓ cup finely chopped fresh parsley

Slow Cooker Directions

1. Combine broth, barley, onion, cranberries, almonds, sage and garlic-pepper seasoning in slow cooker.

2. Spray large nonstick skillet with cooking spray. Heat over medium heat until hot. Brown turkey breast on all sides; add to slow cooker. Cover; cook on LOW 3 to 4 hours or until internal temperature of turkey reaches 170°F when tested with meat thermometer inserted into thickest part of breast, not touching bone.

3. Transfer turkey to cutting board; cover with foil and let stand 10 to 15 minutes before carving. Internal temperature will rise 5°F to 10°F during stand time. Stir parsley into sauce mixture in slow cooker. Serve sliced turkey with sauce and stuffing.

Makes 6 servings

Glazed Roast Pork Loin with Cranberry Stuffing

1¼ cups chopped fresh or partially thawed frozen cranberries
2 teaspoons sugar
½ cup (1 stick) butter or margarine
1 cup chopped onion
1 package (8 ounces) herb-seasoned stuffing mix
1 cup chicken broth
½ cup peeled and diced orange
1 egg, beaten
½ teaspoon grated orange peel
1 (2½- to 3-pound) boneless center cut pork loin roast
¼ cup currant jelly
1 tablespoon cranberry liqueur or cassis

1. Toss cranberries with sugar in small bowl; set aside. Melt butter in saucepan over medium heat until foamy. Add onion; cook and stir until tender. Remove from heat. Combine stuffing mix, broth, orange, egg and orange peel. Add cranberry mixture and onion; toss lightly.

2. Preheat oven to 325°F. To butterfly roast, cut lengthwise down roast almost to, but not through, bottom. Open like a book. Cover roast with plastic wrap; pound with flat side of meat mallet. Remove plastic wrap; spread roast with ¼ of stuffing. Close halves together and tie roast with cotton string at 2-inch intervals. Place leftover stuffing in covered casserole; bake with roast during last 45 minutes of cooking time. Place roast on meat rack in foil-lined roasting pan. Insert meat thermometer into pork.

3. Combine jelly and liqueur. Brush half of mixture over roast after first 45 minutes of roasting. Roast 30 minutes more or until internal temperature reaches 165°F when tested with meat thermometer inserted into thickest part of roast. Brush with remaining jelly mixture. Transfer roast to cutting board; cover with foil. Let stand 10 to 15 minutes before carving. Internal temperature will continue to rise 5°F to 10°F during stand time. Carve roast crosswise; serve with stuffing.

Makes 8 to 10 servings

Oven Roasted Pork & "Two" Potatoes

¾ cup LAWRY'S® Herb & Garlic Marinade with Lemon Juice, divided
1 teaspoon dried thyme
2 pounds pork tenderloin
1 tablespoon BERTOLLI® Olive Oil
½ pound sweet potatoes or yams, peeled and diagonally sliced ½-inch thick
¾ pound red potatoes, unpeeled and cut into 2-inch chunks
1 large onion, peeled and sliced into 1-inch wedges

In small bowl, mix together Herb & Garlic Marinade and thyme; reserve ¼ cup of mixture for basting. Pierce pork deeply with fork in several places. In large resealable plastic bag, add ¼ cup of marinade mixture and pork; seal bag. Marinate in refrigerator
for 30 minutes. Remove pork from bag, discarding used marinade. In large bowl or another large resealable plastic bag, combine oil, sweet potatoes, red potatoes, onion and ¼ cup of marinade mixture; toss to coat. On bottom of foil lined broiler pan, place pork in center and surround with potato mixture. Roast in preheated 450°F oven for 20 minutes. Brush pork and potatoes with remaining ¼ cup of marinade mixture, turning pork over to brush. Return pan to oven and continue roasting until pork reaches internal temperature of 150°F, about 15 to 20 minutes longer.

Makes 4 to 6 servings

Prep. Time: 12 to 15 minutes
Marinate Time: 30 minutes
Cook Time: 35 to 40 minutes

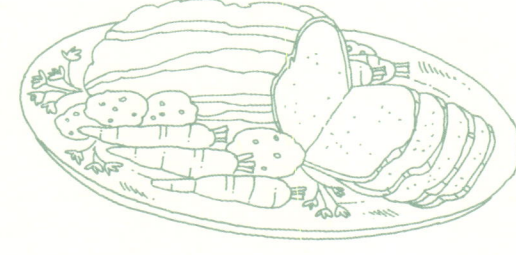

Herb-Crusted Roast Beef and Potatoes

1 (4½-pound) eye of round or sirloin tip beef roast
¾ cup plus 2 tablespoons FILIPPO BERIO® Olive Oil, divided
    Salt and freshly ground black pepper
2 tablespoons paprika
2 pounds small red skin potatoes, cut into halves
1 cup dry bread crumbs
1 teaspoon dried thyme leaves
1 teaspoon dried rosemary
½ teaspoon salt
¼ teaspoon freshly ground black pepper

Preheat oven to 325°F. Brush roast with 2 tablespoons olive oil. Season to taste with salt and pepper. Place in large roasting pan; insert meat thermometer into center of thickest part of roast. Roast 45 minutes.

Meanwhile, in large bowl, combine ½ cup olive oil and paprika. Add potatoes; toss until lightly coated. In small bowl, combine bread crumbs, thyme, rosemary, ½ teaspoon salt, ¼ teaspoon pepper and remaining ¼ cup olive oil.

Carefully remove roast from oven. Place potatoes around roast. Press bread crumb mixture onto top of roast to form crust. Sprinkle any remaining bread crumb mixture over potatoes. Roast an additional 40 to 45 minutes or until meat thermometer registers 145°F for medium-rare or until desired doneness is reached. Transfer roast to carving board; tent with foil. Let stand 5 to 10 minutes before carving. Cut into ¼-inch-thick slices. Serve immediately with potatoes, spooning any bread crumb mixture from roasting pan onto meat.   *Makes 8 servings*

Peppered Pork Chops with Sweet-Sour Cabbage & Cinnamon Applesauce

4 boneless top loin pork chops (4 ounces each) ½-inch thick, trimmed of
   visible fat
1 teaspoon black pepper
4 cups ready-to-use shredded cabbage slaw
4 cups water
¼ cup balsamic vinegar
2 packets sucralose-based sugar substitute*
2 cups unsweetened applesauce
2 teaspoons cinnamon

Sold as the brand name Splenda®.

1. Rinse pork chops; pat dry. Sprinkle tops with pepper. Set aside.

2. Spray small nonstick skillet with nonstick cooking spray and heat over medium-high heat. Add cabbage and cook, stirring, until cabbage starts to brown, about 5 minutes. Do not burn. Add water; cover pan tightly; reduce heat and cook for 20 minutes.

3. Add vinegar and sugar substitute. Stir to mix. Cook to evaporate liquid, about 5 minutes. Cover; keep warm.

4. Spray small nonstick skillet with nonstick cooking spray and heat over medium-high heat. Cook pork chops, just until cooked through, about 5 minutes, turning once.

5. Serve pork chops with cabbage and applesauce sprinkled with cinnamon.

Makes 4 servings

Cream Cheese Chicken with Broccoli

4 pounds boneless skinless chicken breasts, cut into ½-inch pieces
1 tablespoon olive oil
1 package (1 ounce) Italian salad dressing mix
2 cups sliced mushrooms
1 cup chopped onion
1 can (10¾ ounces) condensed low-fat cream of chicken soup, undiluted
1 bag (10 ounces) frozen broccoli florets, thawed
1 package (8 ounces) reduced-fat cream cheese, cubed
¼ cup dry sherry

Slow Cooker Directions

1. Toss chicken with olive oil. Sprinkle with Italian salad dressing mix. Place in slow cooker. Cover; cook on LOW 3 hours.

2. Spray large skillet with nonstick cooking spray. Add mushrooms and onion; cook 5 minutes over medium heat or until onions are tender, stirring occasionally.

3. Add soup, broccoli, cream cheese and sherry to saucepan; cook until hot. Transfer to slow cooker. Cover; cook on LOW 1 hour. *Makes 8 servings*

Herbed Chicken over Spinach Fettuccine

  10 ounces uncooked spinach fettuccine
   1 tablespoon olive oil
   8 boneless skinless chicken thighs (1¼ pounds), cut into 1-inch pieces
1½ teaspoons dried oregano leaves
1½ teaspoons dried thyme leaves
   1 cup dry white wine
   ½ cup water
   1 teaspoon chicken bouillon granules
     Pinch sugar
   2 tablespoons cold butter, cut into cubes

1. Cook pasta according to package directions; drain.

2. While pasta is cooking, heat oil in large nonstick skillet over medium heat. Add chicken, oregano and thyme; cook 3 minutes or until chicken is no longer pink in center. Remove chicken; keep warm.

3. Add wine, water, bouillon and sugar to skillet; bring to a boil over high heat, scraping browned bits from bottom of skillet. Boil 2 minutes or until liquid is reduced by half. Gradually stir butter into simmering sauce.

4. Serve chicken over pasta; spoon sauce over chicken and pasta.

Makes 4 servings

Prep and Cook Time: 20 minutes

Beef Tenderloin with Roasted Vegetables

  1 beef tenderloin roast (about 3 pounds), well trimmed
½ cup chardonnay or other dry white wine
½ cup reduced-sodium soy sauce
  2 cloves garlic, sliced
  1 tablespoon fresh rosemary
  1 tablespoon Dijon mustard
  1 teaspoon dry mustard
  1 pound small red or white potatoes, cut into 1-inch pieces
  1 pound brussels sprouts
  1 package (12 ounces) baby carrots
    Fresh rosemary, for garnish (optional)

1. Place tenderloin in large resealable plastic food storage bag. Combine wine, soy sauce, garlic, rosemary, Dijon mustard and dry mustard in small bowl. Pour over tenderloin. Seal bag; turn to coat. Marinate in refrigerator 4 to 12 hours, turning several times.

2. Preheat oven to 425°F. Spray 13×9-inch baking pan with nonstick cooking spray. Place potatoes, brussels sprouts and carrots in pan. Remove tenderloin from marinade. Pour marinade over vegetables; toss to coat well. Cover vegetables with foil. Bake 30 minutes; stir.

3. Place tenderloin on vegetables. Roast, uncovered, 35 to 45 minutes or until internal temperature of tenderloin reaches 135°F for medium-rare to 150°F for medium when tested with meat thermometer inserted into thickest part of tenderloin.

4. Transfer tenderloin to cutting board; cover with foil. Let stand 10 to 15 minutes before carving. Internal temperature will continue to rise 5°F to 10°F during stand time.

5. Stir vegetables; continue to bake if not tender. Slice tenderloin; arrange on serving platter with roasted vegetables. Garnish with fresh rosemary, if desired.

Makes 10 servings

Baked Ham with Apple-Raspberry Sauce

   1 (3-pound) canned ham
   1 cup chopped green apples
   ½ cup SMUCKER'S® Red Raspberry Preserves
   ½ cup SMUCKER'S® Apple Jelly
   ¾ cup apple cider
   1 tablespoon cider vinegar
   2 tablespoons cornstarch
     Endive or parsley sprigs
     Whole crabapples

Bake ham according to package directions.

Mix chopped apples, SMUCKER'S® preserves, and jelly in medium saucepan. Combine cider vinegar and cornstarch; stir into saucepan. Heat to boiling; boil, stirring constantly, until thickened, about 1 minute.

Slice ham and arrange on platter; garnish with endive and crabapples. Serve with sauce. *Makes 8 to 10 servings*

Note: Fresh crabapples are too sour to eat out of hand, but the canned, spiced varieties are delicious with pork and poultry.

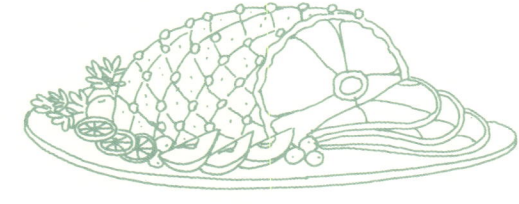

Autumn Vegetables and Pork Chops

    6 pork chops, ¾-inch thick
    1 medium-size acorn squash
 ¾ cup packed brown sugar
    3 tablespoons chopped green onion
    2 tablespoons butter, melted
    2 tablespoons orange juice
    1 teaspoon Worcestershire sauce
    1 teaspoon grated orange peel
 ¼ teaspoon cinnamon
 ⅛ teaspoon nutmeg
    2 cups frozen green peas

Slow Cooker Directions
Slice acorn squash in half, remove seeds and slice each half into 6 slices, approximately ½-inch thick. Place 6 half slices on bottom of 5-quart slow cooker. Arrange 3 pork chops over squash; repeat layers. Combine remaining ingredients except peas; pour over squash mixture. Cover and cook on LOW 5 to 6 hours or until pork and squash are tender. Remove both from slow cooker; keep warm. Stir in frozen peas. Turn heat setting to HIGH. Cover and cook about 5 minutes or until peas are tender; drain.   *Makes 6 servings*

Favorite recipe from **National Pork Board**

Orange-Glazed Salmon

Glaze
- 2 tablespoons soy sauce
- 2 tablespoons orange juice
- 1 tablespoon honey
- ¾ teaspoon grated fresh ginger
- ½ teaspoon rice wine vinegar
- ¼ teaspoon sesame oil

Salmon
- 4 salmon fillets (about 6 ounces each)
- ½ teaspoon salt
- ¼ teaspoon black pepper
- 1 tablespoon olive oil

1. Whisk soy sauce, juice, honey, ginger, vinegar and sesame oil in small mixing bowl; set aside.

2. Season salmon with salt and pepper. Heat olive oil in medium nonstick skillet over high heat. Arrange salmon, skin side up, in skillet. Brush with glaze. Cook salmon 4 minutes or just until center is opaque. Carefully turn; brush with glaze. Cook 4 minutes more. (Salmon will be slightly pink in middle.)

3. Remove salmon from pan to serving plate; cover and keep warm. Place remaining glaze in small saucepan. Simmer and stir until thickened and reduced to about ¼ cup. Spoon glaze over salmon.

Makes 4 servings

Herb Roasted Turkey

1 (12-pound) turkey, thawed if frozen
½ cup FLEISCHMANN'S® Original Margarine, softened, divided
1 tablespoon Italian seasoning

1. Remove neck and giblets from turkey cavities. Rinse turkey; drain well and pat dry. Free legs from tucked position; do not cut band of skin. Using rubber spatula or hand, loosen skin over breast, starting at body cavity opening by legs.

2. Blend 6 tablespoons margarine and Italian seasoning. Spread 2 tablespoons herb mixture inside body cavity; spread remaining herb mixture on meat under skin. Hold skin in place at opening with wooden picks. Return legs to tucked position; turn wings back to hold neck skin in place.

3. Place turkey, breast-side up, on flat rack in shallow open pan. Insert meat thermometer deep into thickest part of thigh next to body, not touching bone. Melt remaining 2 tablespoons margarine; brush over skin.

4. Roast at 325°F for 3½ to 3¾ hours. When skin is golden brown, shield breast loosely with foil to prevent overbrowning. Check for doneness; thigh temperature should be 180°F to 185°F. Transfer turkey to cutting board; let stand 15 to 20 minutes before carving. Remove wooden toothpicks just before carving.

Makes 12 servings

Prep Time: 20 minutes
Cook Time: 3 hours and 30 minutes
Cool Time: 15 minutes
Total Time: 4 hours and 5 minutes

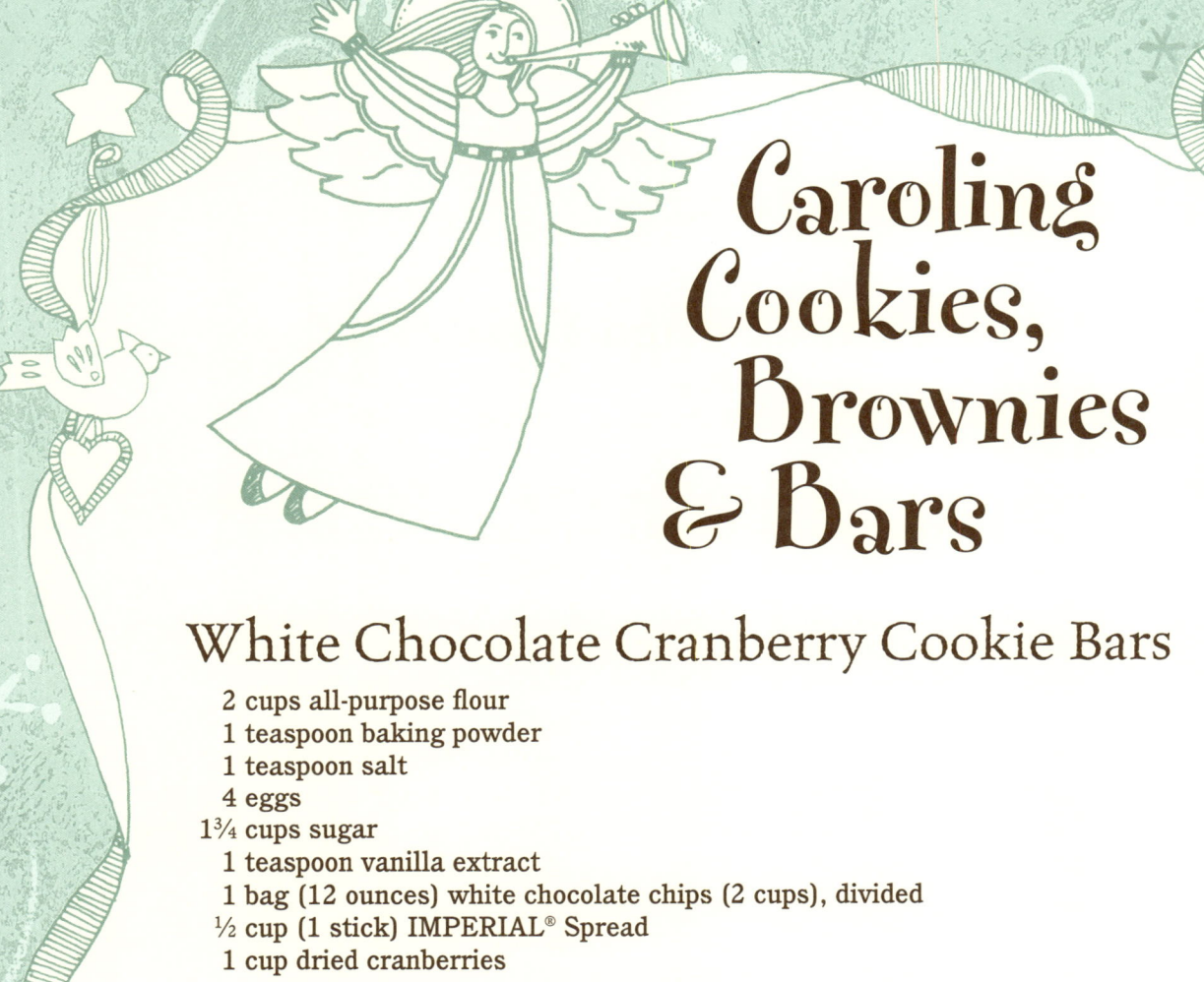

Caroling Cookies, Brownies & Bars

White Chocolate Cranberry Cookie Bars

    2 cups all-purpose flour
    1 teaspoon baking powder
    1 teaspoon salt
    4 eggs
  1¾ cups sugar
    1 teaspoon vanilla extract
    1 bag (12 ounces) white chocolate chips (2 cups), divided
    ½ cup (1 stick) IMPERIAL® Spread
    1 cup dried cranberries

Preheat oven to 350°F. Grease 13×9-inch baking pan; set aside.

In medium bowl, combine flour, baking powder and salt; set aside. In small bowl, with wire whisk, beat eggs, sugar and vanilla; set aside.

In medium saucepan, melt 1 cup white chocolate chips with spread over low heat, stirring occasionally. Remove from heat; let cool slightly. While stirring chocolate mixture, slowly stir in egg mixture, then flour mixture until blended. Stir in remaining 1 cup chips and cranberries. Evenly pour into prepared pan.

Bake uncovered 40 minutes or until center springs back when lightly touched. On wire rack, cool completely. To serve, cut into bars.   *Makes 2 dozen bars*

Spicy Gingerbread Cookies

Cookies
- ¾ cup (1½ sticks) butter, softened
- ⅔ cup light molasses
- ½ cup packed brown sugar
- 1 egg
- 1½ teaspoons grated lemon peel
- 2½ cups all-purpose flour
- 1¼ teaspoons ground cinnamon
- 1 teaspoon ground allspice
- 1 teaspoon vanilla
- ½ teaspoon salt
- ½ teaspoon baking soda
- ½ teaspoon ground ginger
- ¼ teaspoon baking powder

Frosting
- 4 cups powdered sugar
- ½ cup (1 stick) butter, softened
- 4 tablespoons milk
- 2 teaspoons vanilla
- Assorted food colorings (optional)

1. For cookies, combine butter, molasses, brown sugar, egg and lemon peel in large bowl. Beat at medium speed of electric mixer until smooth and creamy. Add all remaining cookie ingredients. Reduce speed to low; beat well. Wrap dough in plastic wrap; refrigerate at least 2 hours.

2. Preheat oven to 350°F. Roll out dough, one half at a time, on well-floured surface to ¼-inch thickness. (Keep remaining dough refrigerated.) Cut with 3- to 4-inch cookie cutters. Place on greased cookie sheets. Bake 6 to 8 minutes or until firm. Remove immediately to wire racks; cool completely.

3. For frosting, combine powdered sugar, butter, milk and vanilla in small bowl. Beat at low speed of electric mixer until fluffy. Tint frosting with food colorings, if desired. Decorate cookies with frosting. *Makes about 4 dozen cookies*

Premier Cheesecake Cranberry Bars

    2 cups all-purpose flour
1½ cups quick or old-fashioned oats
    ¼ cup packed light brown sugar
    1 cup (2 sticks) butter or margarine, softened
    2 cups (12-ounce package) NESTLÉ® TOLL HOUSE® Premier White Morsels
    1 package (8 ounces) cream cheese, softened
    1 can (14 ounces) NESTLÉ® CARNATION® Sweetened Condensed Milk
    ¼ cup lemon juice
    1 teaspoon vanilla extract
    1 can (16 ounces) whole-berry cranberry sauce
    2 tablespoons cornstarch

PREHEAT oven to 350°F. Grease 13×9-inch baking pan.

COMBINE flour, oats and brown sugar in large bowl. Add butter; mix until crumbly. Stir in morsels. Reserve *2½ cups* morsel mixture for topping. With floured fingers, press *remaining* mixture into prepared pan.

BEAT cream cheese in large mixer bowl until creamy. Add sweetened condensed milk, lemon juice and vanilla extract; mix until smooth. Pour over crust. Combine cranberry sauce and cornstarch in medium bowl. Spoon over cream cheese mixture. Sprinkle *reserved* morsel mixture over cranberry mixture.

BAKE for 35 to 40 minutes or until center is set. Cool completely in pan on wire rack. Cover; refrigerate until serving time (up to 1 day). Cut into bars.

Makes 2½ dozen bars

Icicle Ornaments

2½ cups all-purpose flour
¼ teaspoon salt
1 cup sugar
¾ cup (1½ sticks) unsalted butter, softened
2 squares (1 ounce each) white chocolate, melted
1 egg
1 teaspoon vanilla
   Coarse white decorating sugar, colored sugars and decors
   Ribbon

1. Combine flour and salt in medium bowl. Beat sugar and butter in large bowl at medium speed of electric mixer until fluffy. Beat in white chocolate, egg and vanilla. Gradually add flour mixture. Beat at low speed until well blended. Shape dough into disc. Wrap in plastic wrap and refrigerate 30 minutes or until firm.

2. Preheat oven to 350°F. Grease cookie sheets. Shape heaping tablespoonfuls of dough into 10-inch ropes. Fold each rope in half; twist to make icicle shape, leaving opening at top and tapering ends. Roll in coarse sugar; sprinkle with colored sugars and decors as desired. Place 1 inch apart on prepared cookie sheets.

3. Bake 8 to 10 minutes. (Do not brown.) Cool on cookie sheets 1 minute. Remove to wire racks; cool completely. Pull ribbon through opening in top of each icicle; tie small knot in ribbon ends.

Makes about 2½ dozen cookies

Festive Fruited White Chip Blondies

½ cup (1 stick) butter or margarine
1⅔ cups (10-ounce package) HERSHEY'S Premier White Chips, divided
2 eggs
¼ cup granulated sugar
1¼ cups all-purpose flour
⅓ cup orange juice
¾ cup cranberries, chopped
¼ cup chopped dried apricots
½ cup coarsely chopped nuts
¼ cup packed light brown sugar

1. Heat oven to 325°F. Grease and flour 9-inch square baking pan.

2. Melt butter in medium saucepan; stir in 1 cup white chips. Beat eggs in large bowl until foamy. Add granulated sugar; beat until thick and pale yellow in color. Add flour, orange juice and white chip mixture; beat just until combined. Spread one-half of batter, about 1¼ cups, into prepared pan.

3. Bake 15 minutes or until edges are lightly browned; remove from oven.

4. Stir cranberries, apricots and remaining ⅔ cup white chips into remaining one-half of batter; spread over top of hot baked mixture. Stir together nuts and brown sugar; sprinkle over top.

5. Bake 25 to 30 minutes or until edges are lightly browned. Cool completely in pan on wire rack. Cut into bars. *Makes about 16 bars*

Chocolate Peppermint Kisses

  2 egg whites
¼ teaspoon salt
¾ cup sugar
½ cup semisweet chocolate chips
  5 peppermint-flavored hard candies, finely crushed
½ teaspoon vanilla
    Chocolate sprinkles

1. Preheat oven to 250°F. Grease cookie sheets.

2. Beat egg whites and salt at high speed of electric mixer until very stiff, but not dry. Gradually add sugar, beating 5 minutes or until stiff peaks form.

3. Fold in chocolate chips, peppermint candy and vanilla. Drop dough by teaspoonfuls onto prepared cookie sheets. Top each cookie with chocolate sprinkles.

4. Bake 45 minutes or until dry and crisp. Cool 5 minutes on cookie sheets. Remove to wire racks; cool completely. *Makes about 5 dozen cookies*

Thumbprint Cookies

½ cup butter or margarine
¼ cup brown sugar, firmly packed
½ teaspoon vanilla extract
 1 egg, separated
 1 cup all-purpose flour
¼ teaspoon salt
¾ cup finely chopped nuts
 1 (12-ounce) can SOLO® Date or Apricot Filling

Preheat oven to 375°F.

Cream butter or margarine, brown sugar, and vanilla together. Stir in egg yolk and mix well. Stir in flour and salt. With lightly floured fingers, roll dough into balls about 1 inch in diameter. Beat egg white slightly. Dip cookie dough balls into egg white and roll in nuts.

Place on ungreased baking sheet. Press thumb into center of each cookie. Fill depression in cookie with desired filling. Bake 12 to 15 minutes, or until lightly browned and set. Remove from baking sheet and cool on wire rack. Add more filling, if desired, before serving cookies.   *Makes about 2 dozen cookies*

Tip: These cookies can be baked without filling and filled when they are cool. If you choose to follow this method, press depressions in cookies again when they are removed from the oven to allow enough room for the filling.

Orange Cranberry Cookies

¼ cup stick butter or margarine
 1 egg
 3 tablespoons frozen orange juice concentrate
¾ cup all-purpose flour, sifted
⅓ cup EQUAL® SPOONFUL*
¼ cup quick oats, uncooked
 1 teaspoon grated orange peel
¼ teaspoon baking soda
⅛ teaspoon cream of tartar
    Dash salt
½ cup dried cranberries
½ cup chopped walnuts

May substitute 8 packets Equal® sweetener.

• Beat butter in medium bowl. Beat in egg and frozen orange juice concentrate.

• Combine flour, Equal®, oats, orange peel, baking soda, cream of tartar and salt in separate bowl.

• Add flour mixture to butter mixture and mix well. Stir in cranberries and walnuts.

• Drop by rounded teaspoonfuls onto ungreased baking sheet.

• Bake in preheated 375°F oven 8 to 10 minutes or until bottoms are lightly browned. Cool on wire racks.   *Makes 24 cookies*

Chocolate Sugar Spritz

2 squares (1 ounce each) unsweetened chocolate, coarsely chopped
2¼ cups all-purpose flour
¼ teaspoon salt
1 cup (2 sticks) butter, softened
¾ cup granulated sugar
1 egg
1 teaspoon almond extract
½ cup powdered sugar
1 teaspoon ground cinnamon

1. Preheat oven to 400°F.

2. Melt chocolate in small heavy saucepan over low heat, stirring constantly. Combine flour and salt in small bowl; stir to combine.

3. Beat butter and granulated sugar in large bowl at medium speed of electric mixer until light and fluffy. Beat in egg and almond extract. Beat in chocolate. Gradually add flour mixture with mixing spoon. (Dough will be stiff.)

4. Fit cookie press with desired plate (change plates for different shapes after first batch, if desired). Fill press with dough; press dough 1 inch apart on ungreased cookie sheets.

5. Bake 7 minutes or until just set. Combine powdered sugar and cinnamon in small bowl. Transfer to fine-mesh seive and sprinkle over hot cookies while they are still on cookie sheets. Remove cookies to wire racks; cool completely.

6. Store tightly covered at room temperature. These cookies do not freeze well.

Makes 4 to 5 dozen cookies

Almond-Orange Shortbread

1 cup (4 ounces) sliced almonds, divided
2 cups all-purpose flour
1 cup (2 sticks) cold butter, cut into pieces
½ cup sugar
½ cup cornstarch
2 tablespoons grated orange peel
1 teaspoon almond extract

1. Preheat oven to 350°F. To toast almonds, spread ¾ cup almonds in single layer in large baking pan. Bake 6 minutes or until golden brown, stirring frequently. Cool completely in pan. *Reduce oven temperature to 325°F.*

2. Place toasted almonds in food processor. Process using on/off pulses until almonds are coarsely chopped.

3. Add flour, butter, sugar, cornstarch, orange peel and almond extract to food processor. Process using on/off pulses until mixture resembles coarse crumbs.

4. Press dough firmly and evenly into 10×8½-inch rectangle on large ungreased cookie sheet with fingers. Score dough into 1¼-inch squares with knife. Press one slice of remaining almonds in center of each square.

5. Bake 30 to 40 minutes or until shortbread is firm when pressed and lightly browned.

6. Immediately cut into squares along score lines with sharp knife. Remove cookies to wire racks; cool completely.

7. Store loosely covered at room temperature up to 1 week.

Makes about 5 dozen cookies

Chocolate Raspberry Brownies

1⅔ cups (10-ounce package) HERSHEY'S Raspberry Chips
¼ cup (½ stick) butter or margarine
2 eggs
1 teaspoon vanilla extract
1 cup all-purpose flour
½ cup sugar
1 teaspoon baking powder

1. Heat oven to 350°F. Grease 8-inch square baking pan.

2. Combine raspberry chips and butter in medium saucepan. Cook over medium heat, stirring constantly, until melted. Remove from heat. Add eggs and vanilla; stir until well blended. Add flour, sugar and baking powder; stir until well blended. Spread batter into prepared pan.

3. Bake 25 to 30 minutes or until brownies begin to pull away from sides of pan. Cool completely in pan on wire rack. Cut into squares.   *Makes about 20 brownies*

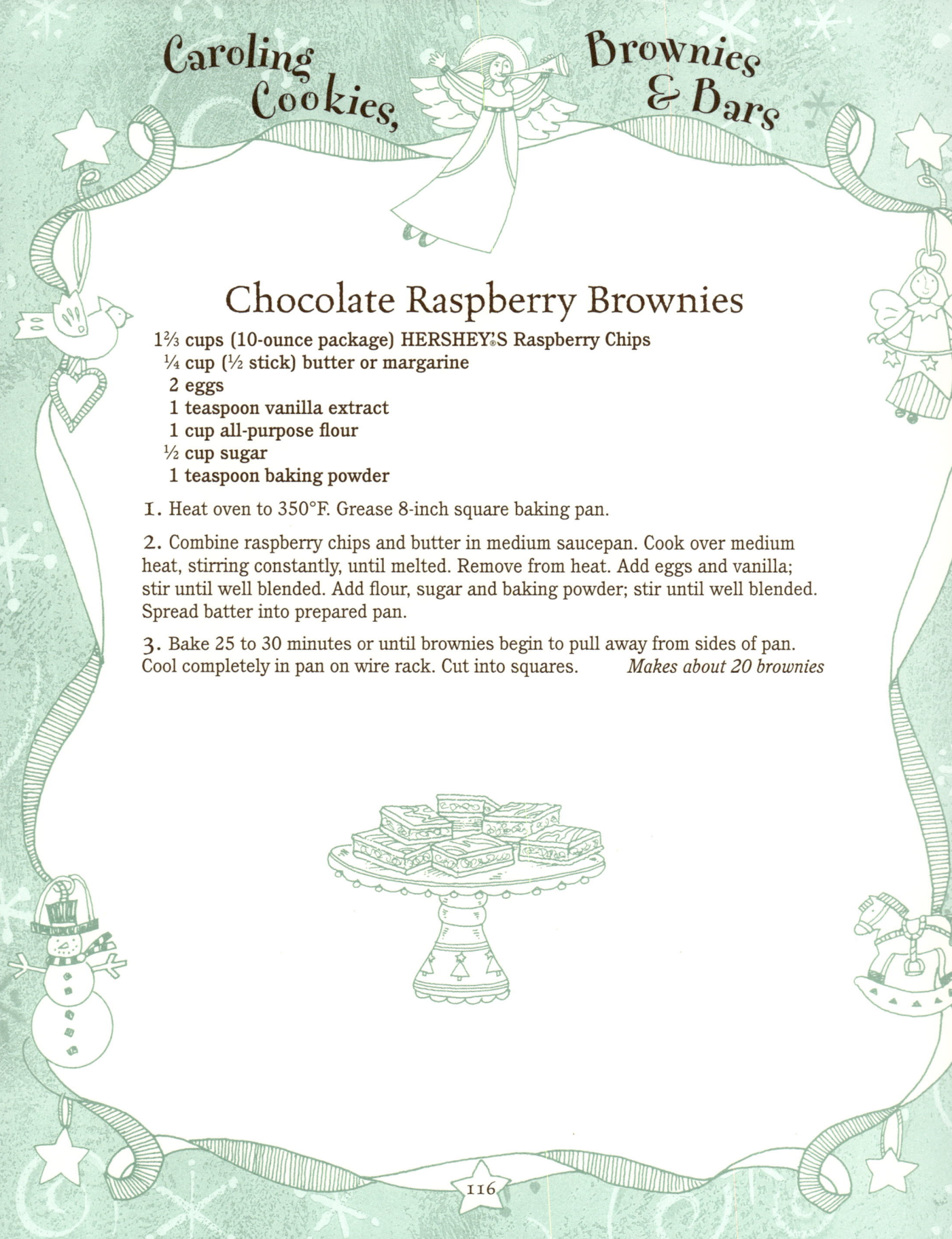

Frosted Butter Cookies

Cookies
  1½ cups (3 sticks) butter, softened
  ¾ cup granulated sugar
  3 egg yolks
  3 cups all-purpose flour
  2 tablespoons orange juice
  1 teaspoon baking powder
  1 teaspoon vanilla

Frosting
  4 cups powdered sugar
  ½ cup (1 stick) butter, softened
  3 to 4 tablespoons milk
  2 teaspoons vanilla
  Food coloring (optional)
  Colored sugars, flaked coconut and cinnamon candies for decoration

1. For cookies, beat 1½ cups butter and granulated sugar in large bowl until creamy. Add egg yolks; beat until light and fluffy. Add flour, orange juice, baking powder and 1 teaspoon vanilla; beat until well mixed. Wrap dough in plastic wrap; refrigerate 2 to 3 hours or until firm.

2. Preheat oven to 350°F. Roll out dough, half at a time, to ¼-inch thickness on well-floured surface. Cut dough with holiday cookie cutters. Place 1 inch apart on ungreased cookie sheets. Bake 6 to 10 minutes or until edges are golden brown. Remove to wire racks; cool completely.

3. For frosting, beat powdered sugar, butter, milk and vanilla in bowl until fluffy. If desired, divide frosting into small bowls and tint with food coloring. Frost cookies; decorate as desired.

Makes about 3 dozen cookies

Jolly Snowman Cookies

½ cup (1 stick) butter, softened
½ cup granulated sugar
 1 teaspoon vanilla extract
 1 cup all-purpose flour
¼ teaspoon salt
 1 cup "M&M's"® Chocolate Mini Baking Bits, divided
    White Icing (recipe follows)

Preheat oven to 375°F. In large bowl cream butter and sugar until light and fluffy; beat in vanilla. In medium bowl combine flour and salt; add to creamed mixture. Stir in ¾ cup "M&M's"® Chocolate Mini Baking Bits. Divide dough into 12 equal sections. Roll each section into 3 balls, large, medium and small for each snowman. Place 3 balls in row, ¼ inch apart on ungreased cookie sheet for each snowman; flatten balls slightly. Bake 12 minutes. Remove from oven. Cool on cookie sheets 1 to 2 minutes; cool completely on wire racks. Prepare White Icing; pour over cookies. Let cookies stand about 10 minutes or until almost set. Decorate with remaining ¼ cup "M&M's"® Chocolate Mini Baking Bits to look like snowmen. Store in tightly covered container.

Makes 1 dozen cookies

White Icing: In small bowl combine 1½ cups powdered sugar and 1 tablespoon milk until well blended. Add additional milk, 1 teaspoon at a time, if necessary to make frosting pourable.

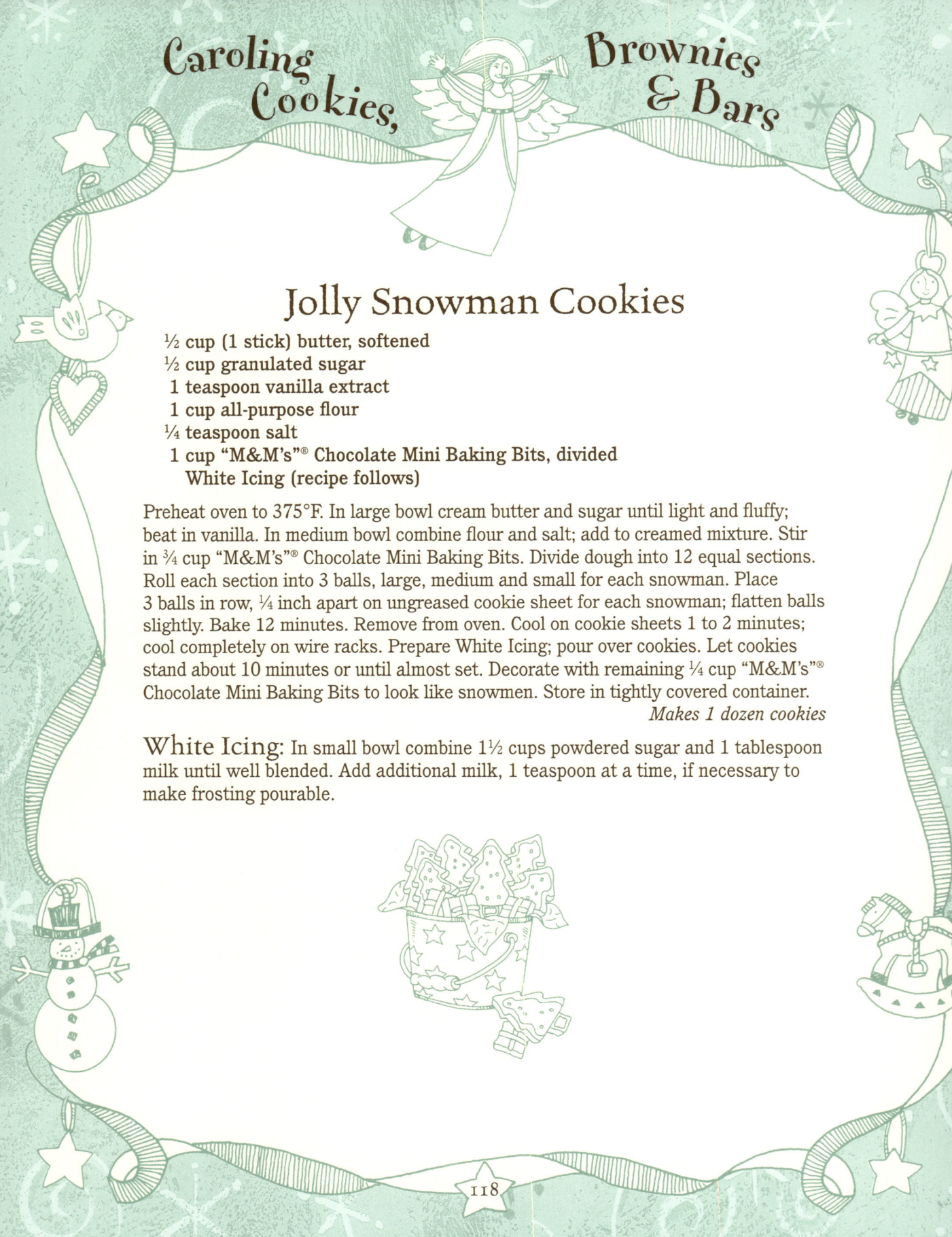

Raspberry-Glazed Brownies with Cheesecake Topping

¾ cup all-purpose flour
14 packets aspartame sugar substitute*, divided
¼ cup cocoa powder
¾ teaspoon baking powder
⅛ teaspoon salt
1 jar (2½ ounces) puréed prunes
¼ cup cold coffee or fat-free (skim) milk
2 tablespoons canola oil
1 large egg
¾ teaspoon vanilla, divided
¼ cup seedless raspberry all-fruit spread
2 ounces reduced-fat cream cheese
1½ tablespoons fat-free (skim) milk

*Aspartame-based sugar substitutes are sold under the brand names Equal®, NutraSweet® and NatraTaste®.

1. Preheat oven to 350°F.

2. Combine flour, 12 packets sugar substitute, cocoa, baking powder and salt in large bowl; stir until well blended. Combine prunes, coffee, oil, egg and ½ teaspoon vanilla in medium bowl; stir until well blended. Make well in center of dry ingredients; add prune mixture. Stir until just blended.

3. Spread batter evenly in 8×8-inch square nonstick baking pan. Bake 8 minutes. (Brownies will not appear to be done.) Cool completely in pan on wire rack.

4. Meanwhile, place raspberry spread in small microwavable bowl. Microwave at HIGH 10 seconds; stir until smooth. Brush evenly over brownies with pastry brush.

5. Combine cream cheese, 1½ tablespoons milk, remaining 2 packets sugar substitute and ¼ teaspoon vanilla in medium bowl. Beat at medium speed of electric mixer until well blended and smooth. Top each brownie with 1 teaspoon cream cheese mixture.   *Makes 12 brownies*

Chocolate-Dipped Walnut Biscotti

1¼ cups granulated sugar
1 Butter Flavor CRISCO® Stick or 1 cup Butter Flavor CRISCO®
  all-vegetable shortening
2 eggs
¼ cup light corn syrup or regular pancake syrup
1 tablespoon vanilla
3 cups all-purpose flour
¾ teaspoon baking powder
½ teaspoon baking soda
½ teaspoon salt
1 cup walnuts, coarsely chopped
1 package (8 ounces) white chocolate, coarsely chopped
  Red and green food color

1. Heat oven to 350°F. Place sheets of foil on countertop for cooling cookies.

2. Combine sugar and shortening in large bowl. Beat at medium speed of electric mixer until well blended. Add eggs, syrup and vanilla. Beat until well blended and fluffy.

3. Combine flour, baking powder, baking soda and salt. Add gradually to creamed mixture at low speed. Mix until well blended. Stir in walnuts.

4. Divide dough in half. Shape each half of dough into a log 2½ inches wide, 1-inch high and 9-inches long. Place on ungreased baking sheet.

5. Bake one log at a time at 350°F for 17 minutes. Remove log from oven. Cool 10 minutes on baking sheet. Cut diagonally into 1-inch wide cookies. Place cookies on their sides on baking sheet. Bake for an additional 8 to 10 minutes. DO NOT OVERBAKE. Cool 2 minutes on baking sheet. Remove cookies to foil to cool completely.

6. Place chocolate pieces in a microwave-safe bowl. Microwave at 100% (HIGH) 30 seconds. Stir. Repeat at 30 second intervals until melted. Divide melted chocolate into two bowls. Add food coloring, red in one bowl, green in the other, drop by drop, until desired shade is reached. Dip one end of half of cookies into red chocolate and the other half into green chocolate. Allow to set completely.   *Makes about 2 dozen*

Gingerbread Cookies

½ cup shortening
⅓ cup packed light brown sugar
¼ cup dark molasses
 1 egg white
½ teaspoon vanilla
1½ cups all-purpose flour
 1 teaspoon ground cinnamon
½ teaspoon baking soda
½ teaspoon salt
½ teaspoon ground ginger
¼ teaspoon baking powder

1. Beat shortening, brown sugar, molasses, egg white and vanilla in large bowl at high speed of electric mixer until smooth. Combine flour, cinnamon, baking soda, salt, ginger and baking powder in small bowl. Add to shortening mixture; mix well. Wrap dough in plastic wrap; refrigerate until firm, about 4 hours or overnight.

2. Preheat oven to 350°F. Grease cookie sheets.

3. Roll dough on lightly floured surface to ⅛-inch thickness. Cut into desired shapes with cookie cutters. Place on prepared cookie sheets.

4. Bake 6 to 8 minutes or until edges begin to brown. Remove to wire racks; cool completely. *Makes about 2½ dozen cookies*

Mocha Mint Crisps

1 cup (2 sticks) butter or margarine, softened
1 cup sugar
1 egg
¼ cup light corn syrup
¼ teaspoon peppermint extract
1 teaspoon powdered instant coffee
1 teaspoon hot water
2 cups all-purpose flour
6 tablespoons HERSHEY'S Cocoa
2 teaspoons baking soda
¼ teaspoon salt
   Mocha Mint Sugar (recipe follows)

1. Beat butter and sugar in large bowl until fluffy. Add egg, corn syrup and peppermint extract; beat until well blended. Dissolve instant coffee in hot water; stir into butter mixture.

2. Stir together flour, cocoa, baking soda and salt; gradually add to butter mixture, beating until well blended. Cover; refrigerate dough until firm enough to shape into balls.

3. Heat oven to 350°F.

4. Shape dough into 1-inch balls. Roll balls in Mocha Mint Sugar. Place on ungreased cookie sheet, about 2 inches apart.

5. Bake 8 to 10 minutes or until no imprint remains when touched lightly. Cool slightly; remove from cookie sheet to wire rack. Cool completely.

Makes about 4 dozen cookies

Mocha Mint Sugar: Stir together ¼ cup powdered sugar, 2 tablespoons finely crushed hard peppermint candies (about 6 candies) and 1½ teaspoons powdered instant coffee in small bowl.

Pumpkin Cheesecake Squares

1½ cups gingersnap crumbs, plus extra for garnish
6 tablespoons butter, melted
2 eggs
¼ cup plus 2 tablespoons sugar, divided
2½ teaspoons vanilla, divided
1 (8-ounce) package plus 1 (3-ounce) package cream cheese, softened and divided
1¼ cups solid-pack pumpkin
1 teaspoon ground cinnamon
¼ teaspoon ground ginger
¼ teaspoon ground nutmeg
¼ teaspoon ground cloves
1 cup sour cream

1. Preheat oven to 325°F. Lightly grease 13×9-inch baking pan. Combine gingersnap crumbs and butter in small bowl until crumbly. Press into bottom of prepared baking pan. Bake 10 minutes.

2. Combine eggs, ¼ cup sugar and 1½ teaspoons vanilla in blender or food processor. Process about 1 minute, until smooth. Add cream cheese and pumpkin; process until thoroughly blended. Stir in spices. Pour mixture evenly over hot crust. Bake 40 minutes.

3. For topping, whisk sour cream, remaining 2 tablespoons sugar and 1 teaspoon vanilla until blended. Remove pan from oven; spread sour cream mixture evenly over cheesecake surface. Bake 5 minutes. Turn off oven; open door halfway and let pan cool in oven. When cool, refrigerate 2 hours. Sprinkle with extra gingersnap crumbs; cut into 1-inch squares. *Makes 35 (1-inch) squares*

White Chocolate & Almond Brownies

½ cup (1 stick) unsalted butter
8 ounces white chocolate
3 eggs
¾ cup sugar
1 cup all-purpose flour
1 teaspoon vanilla
¼ teaspoon salt
½ cup slivered almonds

1. Preheat oven to 325°F. Lightly grease 9-inch square pan. Melt butter in medium saucepan over low heat; do not let butter turn brown. Remove from heat; add white chocolate. Swirl butter to cover chocolate; *do not stir.*

2. Beat eggs 30 seconds in large bowl. Gradually beat in sugar; continue beating 2 to 3 minutes or until mixture turns pale yellow. Beat in chocolate mixture, flour, vanilla and salt just until smooth. Pour batter evenly into prepared pan; sprinkle with almonds. Bake 35 to 40 minutes or until center is completely set. If necessary, cover pan loosely with foil during last 10 minutes of baking to prevent overbrowning. Cool completely in pan on wire rack. Cut into 2-inch squares.

Makes about 16 brownies

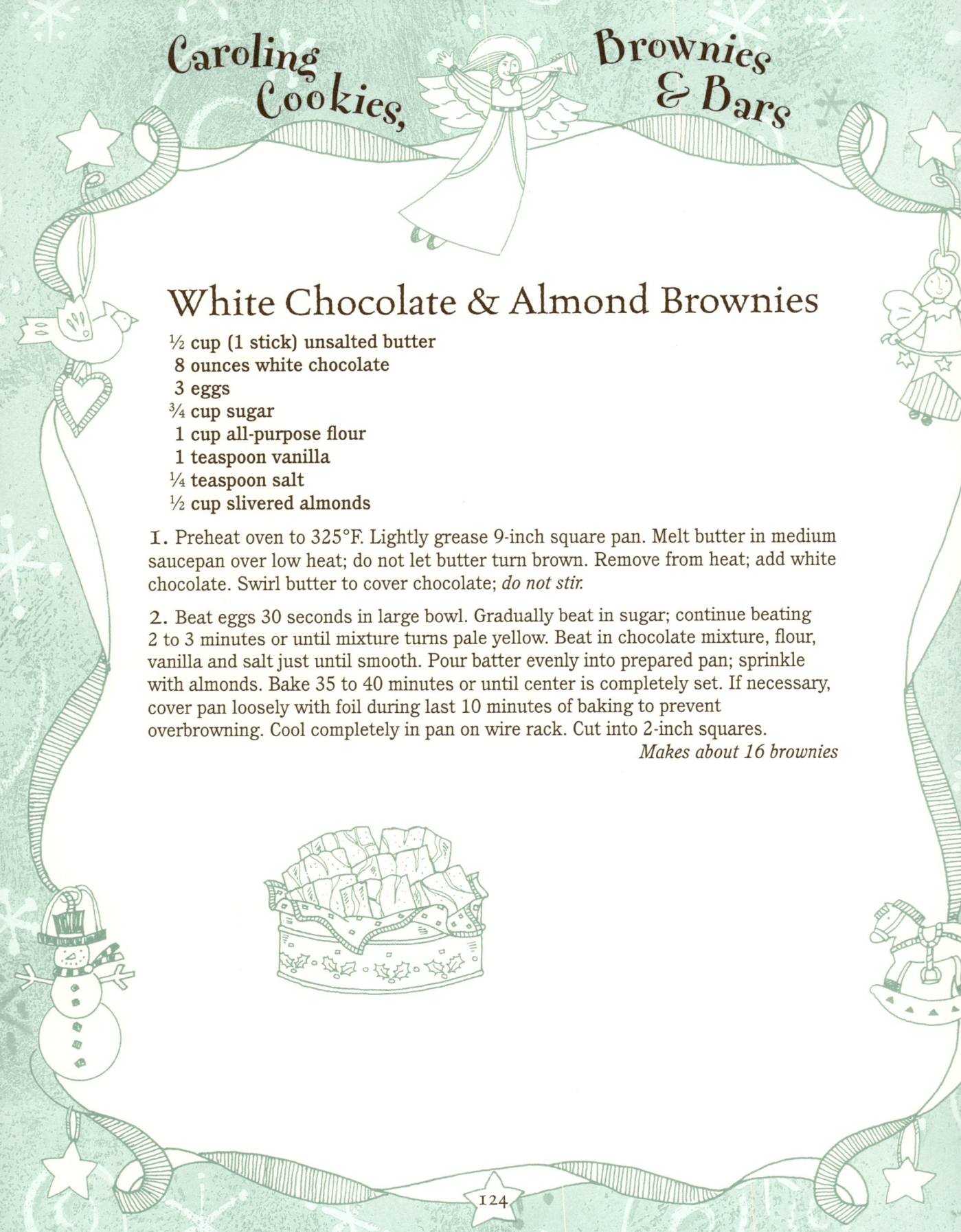

Moist Pumpkin Cookies

½ cup (1 stick) butter, softened
1 cup packed brown sugar
½ cup granulated sugar
1½ cups solid-pack pumpkin (not pumpkin pie filling)
1 egg
1 teaspoon vanilla
2¼ cups all-purpose flour
1¼ teaspoons ground cinnamon
1 teaspoon baking powder
½ teaspoon baking soda
½ teaspoon salt
½ teaspoon ground nutmeg
¾ cup raisins
½ cup chopped walnuts
Powdered Sugar Glaze (recipe follows)

1. Preheat oven to 350°F. Beat butter and sugars in large bowl until creamy. Beat in pumpkin, egg and vanilla until light and fluffy. Mix in flour, cinnamon, baking powder, baking soda, salt and nutmeg until blended. Stir in raisins and walnuts. Drop heaping tablespoonfuls of dough 2 inches apart onto ungreased cookie sheets.

2. Bake 12 to 15 minutes or until set. Cool 2 minutes on cookie sheets. Remove to wire racks; cool completely. Prepare Powdered Sugar Glaze. Drizzle glaze over cookies. Let glaze set. Store between layers of waxed paper in airtight containers.

Makes about 3½ dozen cookies

Powdered Sugar Glaze: Combine 1 cup powdered sugar and 2 tablespoons milk in small bowl until well blended.

Cheery Cheesecake Cookie Bars

4 bars (1 ounce each) HERSHEY'S Unsweetened Baking Chocolate,
  broken into pieces
1 cup (2 sticks) butter
2½ cups sugar, divided
4 eggs, divided
1 teaspoon vanilla extract
2 cups all-purpose flour
1 package (8 ounces) cream cheese, softened
1¾ cups (10-ounce package) HERSHEY'S MINI KISSES™ Milk Chocolate
    or Semi-Sweet Chocolates, divided
½ cup chopped red or green maraschino cherries
½ teaspoon almond extract
   Few drops red food color (optional)

1. Heat oven to 350°F. Grease 13×9×2-inch baking pan.

2. Place baking chocolate and butter in large microwave-safe bowl. Microwave at HIGH (100%) 2 to 2½ minutes, stirring after each minute, until mixture is melted. Beat in 2 cups sugar, 3 eggs and vanilla until blended. Stir in flour; spread batter into prepared pan.

3. Beat cream cheese, remaining ½ cup sugar and remaining egg; stir in 1¼ cups Mini Kisses™, cherries, almond extract and red food color, if desired. Drop by spoonfuls over top of chocolate mixture in pan.

4. Bake 35 to 40 minutes or just until set. Remove from oven; immediately sprinkle remaining ½ cup Mini Kisses™ over top. Cool completely in pan on wire rack; cut into bars. Cover; refrigerate leftover bars. *Makes 36 bars*

Raspberry Pecan Thumbprints

    2 cups all-purpose flour
    1 cup pecan pieces, finely chopped and divided
    ½ teaspoon ground cinnamon
    ¼ teaspoon ground allspice
    ⅛ teaspoon salt
    1 cup (2 sticks) butter, softened
    ½ cup packed light brown sugar
    2 teaspoons vanilla
    ⅓ cup seedless raspberry jam

1. Preheat oven to 350°F. Combine flour, ½ cup pecans, cinnamon, allspice and salt in medium bowl.

2. Beat butter in large bowl at medium speed of electric mixer until smooth. Gradually beat in brown sugar; beat until light and fluffy. Beat in vanilla until blended. Beat in flour mixture just until blended.

3. Shape dough into 1-inch balls; flatten slightly and place on ungreased cookie sheets. Press down with thumb in center of each ball to form indentation. Pinch together any cracks in dough. Fill each indentation with generous ¼ teaspoon jam. Sprinkle filled cookies with remaining ½ cup pecans.

4. Bake 14 minutes or until just set. Let cookies stand on cookie sheets 5 minutes. Transfer to wire racks to cool completely. Store in airtight container at room temperature. Cookies are best the day after baking.   *Makes 3 dozen cookies*

Holiday Fruit Drops

½ cup (1 stick) butter, softened
¾ cup packed brown sugar
1 egg
1¼ cups all-purpose flour
1 teaspoon vanilla
½ teaspoon baking soda
½ teaspoon ground cinnamon
    Pinch salt
1 cup (8 ounces) diced candied pineapple
1 cup (8 ounces) whole red and green candied cherries
1 cup (8 ounces) chopped pitted dates
1 cup (6 ounces) semisweet chocolate chips
½ cup whole hazelnuts
½ cup pecan halves
½ cup coarsely chopped walnuts

1. Preheat oven to 325°F. Lightly grease cookie sheets or line with parchment paper. Beat butter and brown sugar in large bowl at medium speed of electric mixer. Beat in egg until light and fluffy. Mix in flour, vanilla, baking soda, cinnamon and salt. Stir in pineapple, cherries, dates, chocolate chips, hazelnuts, pecans and walnuts. Drop dough by rounded teaspoonfuls 2 inches apart onto prepared cookie sheets.

2. Bake 15 to 20 minutes or until firm and lightly browned around edges. Remove to wire racks to cool completely.   *Makes about 8 dozen cookies*

Cranberry Nut Oatmeal Cookies

1¼ cups firmly packed light brown sugar
¾ Butter Flavor CRISCO® Stick or ¾ cup Butter Flavor CRISCO all-vegetable
    shortening plus additional for greasing
1 egg
⅓ cup milk
1½ teaspoons vanilla
1 teaspoon grated orange peel
3 cups quick oats, uncooked
1 cup all-purpose flour
½ teaspoon baking soda
½ teaspoon salt
¼ teaspoon cinnamon
1 cup dried cranberries
1 cup coarsely chopped walnuts

1. Heat oven to 375°F. Grease baking sheets. Place sheets of foil on countertop for cooling cookies.

2. Place brown sugar, ¾ cup shortening, egg, milk, vanilla and orange peel in large bowl. Beat at medium speed of electric mixer until well blended.

3. Combine oats, flour, baking soda, salt and cinnamon. Add to shortening mixture; beat at low speed just until blended. Stir in cranberries and walnuts.

4. Drop dough by rounded tablespoonfuls 2 inches apart onto prepared baking sheets.

5. Bake one baking sheet at a time at 375°F for 10 to 12 minutes or until cookies are lightly browned. *Do not overbake.* Cool 2 minutes on baking sheet. Remove cookies to foil to cool completely.   *Makes about 2½ dozen cookies*

Chocolate Cherry-Nut Drops

¾ cup (1½ sticks) butter or margarine, softened
1 cup sugar
1 egg
½ teaspoon vanilla extract
¼ teaspoon almond extract
1¾ cups all-purpose flour
½ cup HERSHEY'S Cocoa
½ teaspoon baking soda
¼ teaspoon salt
⅓ cup water
½ cup chopped nuts
½ cup finely chopped maraschino cherries, well drained
   Vanilla Frosting (page 131)
   Candied cherries, quartered or multi-colored sprinkles (optional)

1. Beat butter and sugar in large bowl until fluffy. Add egg and vanilla and almond extracts; beat until well blended. Stir together flour, cocoa, baking soda and salt; add alternately with water to butter mixture. Stir in nuts and maraschino cherries. Cover; refrigerate dough 2 to 3 hours.

2. Heat oven to 350°F.

3. Lightly grease cookie sheet. Drop dough by slightly heaping teaspoons onto prepared cookie sheet.

4. Bake 9 to 10 minutes or until set. Cool 1 minute; remove from cookie sheet to wire rack. Cool completely. Spread with Vanilla Frosting. Garnish with candied cherries, if desired.   *Makes about 3½ dozen cookies*

Vanilla Frosting

 2 tablespoons butter or margarine, softened
1½ cups powdered sugar
 1 to 2 tablespoons milk
 ¼ teaspoon vanilla extract
 ⅛ to ¼ teaspoon almond extract

Beat butter until creamy. Gradually add powdered sugar alternately with milk, beating to spreading consistency. Beat in vanilla and almond extracts.

Makes about ¾ cup

Almond Raspberry Macaroons

2 cups BLUE DIAMOND® Blanched Almond Paste
1 cup granulated sugar
6 large egg whites
  Powdered sugar
  Seedless raspberry jam, stirred until smooth

Beat almond paste and granulated sugar until mixture resembles coarse cornmeal. Beat in egg whites, a little at a time, until thoroughly combined. Place heaping teaspoonfuls onto cookie sheet lined with waxed paper or parchment paper. Coat finger with powdered sugar and make an indentation in the middle of each cookie. (Coat finger with powdered sugar each time.) Bake at 350°F for 15 to 20 minutes or until lightly browned. Remove from oven and fill each indentation with about ¼ teaspoon raspberry jam. Cool. If using waxed paper, carefully peel paper off cookies when cooled.

Makes about 30 cookies

Chocolate Chip Cranberry Cheese Bars

1 cup (2 sticks) butter or margarine, softened
1 cup packed brown sugar
2 cups all-purpose flour
1½ cups quick or old-fashioned oats
2 teaspoons grated orange peel
2 cups (12-ounce package) NESTLÉ® TOLL HOUSE® Semi-Sweet
    Chocolate Morsels
1 cup (4 ounces) sweetened dried cranberries
1 package (8 ounces) cream cheese, softened
1 can (14 ounces) NESTLÉ® CARNATION® Sweetened Condensed Milk

PREHEAT oven to 350°F. Grease 13×9-inch baking pan.

BEAT butter and sugar in large mixer bowl until creamy. Gradually beat in flour, oats and orange peel until crumbly. Stir in morsels and cranberries; reserve *2 cups* mixture. Press *remaining* mixture onto bottom of prepared baking pan.

BAKE for 15 minutes. Beat cream cheese in small mixer bowl until smooth. Gradually beat in sweetened condensed milk. Pour over hot crust; sprinkle with reserved mixture. Bake for 25 to 30 minutes or until center is set. Cool in pan on wire rack. Cut into bars. *Makes about 3 dozen bars*

Holiday Thumbprint Cookies

1 package (8 ounces) sugar-free low-fat yellow cake mix
3 tablespoons orange juice
2 teaspoons grated orange peel
½ teaspoon vanilla
5 teaspoons strawberry all-fruit spread
2 tablespoons pecans, chopped

1. Preheat oven to 350°F. Spray baking sheets with nonstick cooking spray.

2. Beat cake mix, orange juice, orange peel and vanilla in medium bowl at medium speed of electric mixer 2 minutes or until mixture looks crumbly. Increase speed to medium-high and beat 2 minutes or until smooth dough forms. (Dough will be very sticky.)

3. Coat hands with nonstick cooking spray. Roll dough into 1-inch balls. Place balls 2½ inches apart on prepared baking sheets. Press center of each ball with thumb. Fill each thumbprint with ¼ teaspoon fruit spread. Sprinkle with nuts.

4. Bake 8 to 9 minutes or until cookies are light golden brown and no longer shiny. *Do not overbake.* Remove to wire racks; cool completely.   *Makes 20 cookies*

Cranberry Brown Sugar Cookies

2 cups firmly packed DOMINO® Dark Brown Sugar
1 cup butter or margarine, softened
2 eggs
½ cup sour cream
3½ cups all-purpose flour
1 teaspoon baking soda
1 teaspoon salt
1 teaspoon ground cinnamon
½ teaspoon ground nutmeg
¼ teaspoon ground cloves
1 cup dried cranberries (5 ounces)
1 cup golden raisins

Heat oven to 400°F. Lightly grease cookie sheets. Beat sugar and butter in large bowl until light and fluffy. Add eggs and sour cream; beat until creamy. Stir together flour, baking soda, salt, cinnamon, nutmeg and cloves in small bowl; gradually add to sugar mixture, beating until well mixed. Stir in cranberries and raisins. Drop by rounded teaspoonfuls onto cookie sheets. Bake 8 to 10 minutes or until lightly browned. Remove from cookie sheets to cooling racks. Cool completely.

Makes about 5 dozen cookies

Reduced Fat Version: Substitute 70% spread margarine for butter, ½ cup refrigerated or frozen non-fat egg product, thawed, for the 2 eggs, and non-fat sour cream for the sour cream. Proceed as directed. Per cookie: 87 calories, 2g fat.

Tips: 1 cup chopped dried cherries may be substituted for 1 cup dried cranberries. If cranberries are exceptionally large, chop before adding to cookie dough.

Prep Time: 30 minutes
Bake Time: 10 minutes
Cool Time: 30 minutes

Primo Pumpkin Brownies

¾ cup packed brown sugar
½ cup (1 stick) unsalted butter, softened
1 teaspoon vanilla
1 egg
1⅓ cups all-purpose flour
1 cup solid-pack pumpkin (not pumpkin pie filling)
2 teaspoons pumpkin pie spice
1 teaspoon baking powder
¼ teaspoon salt
½ cup toffee baking bits
   White Chocolate Cream Cheese Frosting (page 136)

1. Preheat oven to 350°F. Grease 8-inch square baking pan.

2. Beat brown sugar, butter and vanilla at medium speed of electric mixer until smooth. Add egg; beat until fluffy. Stir in flour, pumpkin, pumpkin pie spice, baking powder and salt. Fold in toffee bits. Spread evenly in prepared pan.

3. Bake 40 to 45 minutes or until toothpick inserted near center comes out clean. Cool completely in pan on wire rack.

4. Prepare White Chocolate Cream Cheese Frosting. Frost bars; cut into squares.

Makes 9 brownies

continued on page 136

Primo Pumpkin Brownies, continued

White Chocolate Cream Cheese Frosting

2 tablespoons whipping cream
4 squares (1 ounce each) white chocolate, chopped
6 ounces cream cheese, softened
⅓ cup powdered sugar, sifted

1. Heat cream in small saucepan over medium heat until almost boiling; remove from heat. Add white chocolate stirring constantly until completely melted. Cool slightly.

2. Beat cream cheese and sugar 1 minute at medium speed of electric mixer until fluffy. Beat in chocolate mixture until smooth.   *Makes 2 to 3 cups frosting*

Christmas Spirits

32 chocolate creme sandwich cookies
1¼ cups toasted California walnuts
¾ cup powdered sugar, divided
2 tablespoons instant coffee powder, divided
2 tablespoons light corn syrup
⅓ cup brandy, coffee liqueur or rum

Break up cookies and place in food processor; process until cookies form fine crumbs (about 2 cups crumbs). Add walnuts, ½ cup powdered sugar and 1½ tablespoons coffee powder. Process until thoroughly combined. Add corn syrup; gradually mix in brandy until mixture forms a thick paste. Form into 1-inch balls.

Combine remaining ¼ cup powdered sugar and remaining ½ tablespoon coffee powder. Roll balls in sugar mixture to coat. Cookies may be stored loosely packed between sheets of waxed paper or aluminum foil in airtight container for up to 2 weeks.   *Makes about 48 cookies*

Favorite recipe from **Walnut Marketing Board**

Molasses Spice Cookies

1¾ cups all-purpose flour
1 teaspoon baking soda
1 teaspoon ground ginger
1 teaspoon ground cinnamon
¼ teaspoon ground cloves
¼ teaspoon salt
1 cup granulated sugar
¾ cup (1½ sticks) butter or margarine, softened
1 large egg
¼ cup unsulphured molasses
2 cups (12-ounce package) NESTLÉ® TOLL HOUSE® Premier White Morsels
1 cup finely chopped walnuts

COMBINE flour, baking soda, ginger, cinnamon, cloves and salt in small bowl. Beat sugar and butter in large mixer bowl until creamy. Beat in egg and molasses. Gradually beat in flour mixture. Stir in morsels. Refrigerate for 20 minutes or until slightly firm.

PREHEAT oven to 375°F.

ROLL dough into 1-inch balls; roll in walnuts. Place on ungreased baking sheets.

BAKE for 9 to 11 minutes or until golden brown. Cool on baking sheets for 2 minutes; remove to wire racks to cool completely

Makes about 2½ dozen cookies

Almond Cheesecake Brownies

4 squares (1 ounce each) semisweet chocolate
5 tablespoons butter, divided
1 package (3 ounces) cream cheese, softened
1 cup granulated sugar, divided
3 eggs, divided
½ cup plus 1 tablespoon all-purpose flour
1½ teaspoons vanilla, divided
½ teaspoon baking powder
¼ teaspoon salt
½ teaspoon almond extract
½ cup chopped or slivered almonds
Almond Icing (page 139)

1. Preheat oven to 350°F. Grease 8-inch square baking pan. Melt chocolate and 3 tablespoons butter in small heavy saucepan over low heat; set aside. Mix cream cheese with remaining 2 tablespoons butter in small bowl. Slowly add ¼ cup granulated sugar, blending well. Add 1 egg, 1 tablespoon flour and ½ teaspoon vanilla; set aside. Beat remaining 2 eggs and ¾ cup granulated sugar in large bowl until light and fluffy. Add remaining ½ cup flour, baking powder and salt. Blend in chocolate mixture, remaining 1 teaspoon vanilla and almond extract. Stir in almonds.

2. Spread half the chocolate mixture into prepared pan. Cover with cream cheese mixture; spoon remaining chocolate mixture over top. Swirl with knife or spatula to create marbled effect. Bake 30 to 35 minutes or until center is set. *Do not overbake.* Meanwhile, prepare Almond Icing. Cool brownies 5 minutes; spread icing evenly over top. Cool completely in pan on wire rack. Cut into 2-inch squares.

Makes 16 brownies

Almond Icing

½ cup semisweet chocolate chips
3 tablespoons milk
2 tablespoons butter
¼ teaspoon almond extract
1 cup powdered sugar

Combine chocolate chips, milk, butter and almond extract in small heavy saucepan. Stir over low heat until chocolate is melted. Add powdered sugar; beat until glossy and easy to spread.

Chocolate Cranberry Bars

2 cups vanilla wafer crumbs
½ cup unsweetened cocoa
3 tablespoons sugar
⅔ cup (1⅓ sticks) cold butter, cut into pieces
1 (14-ounce) can EAGLE BRAND® Sweetened Condensed Milk (NOT evaporated milk)
1⅓ cups (6-ounce package) sweetened dried cranberries or raisins
1 cup peanut butter-flavored chips
1 cup finely chopped walnuts

1. Preheat oven to 350°F. In medium mixing bowl, combine wafer crumbs, cocoa and sugar; cut in butter until crumbly.

2. Press mixture evenly on bottom and ½ inch up sides of ungreased 13×9-inch baking pan. Pour Eagle Brand evenly over crumb mixture. Sprinkle evenly with dried cranberries, peanut butter chips and nuts; press down firmly.

3. Bake 25 to 30 minutes or until lightly browned. Cool completely in pan on wire rack. Cover with foil; let stand several hours. Cut into bars. Store covered at room temperature. *Makes about 36 bars*

Prep Time : 15 minutes
Bake Time: 25 to 30 minutes

Spicy Pumpkin Cookies

2 CRISCO® Sticks or 2 cups CRISCO® all-vegetable shortening
2 cups sugar
1 can (16 ounces) solid-pack pumpkin
2 eggs
2 teaspoons vanilla
4 cups all-purpose flour
2 teaspoons baking powder
2 teaspoons ground cinnamon
1 teaspoon salt
1 teaspoon baking soda
1 teaspoon ground nutmeg
½ teaspoon ground allspice
2 cups raisins
1 cup chopped nuts

1. Heat oven to 350°F.

2. Combine shortening, sugar, pumpkin, eggs and vanilla in large bowl; beat well.

3. Combine flour, baking powder, cinnamon, salt, baking soda, nutmeg and allspice in medium bowl. Add to pumpkin mixture; mix well. Stir in raisins and nuts. Drop rounded teaspoonfuls of dough, 2 inches apart, onto greased cookie sheet.

4. Bake at 350°F for 12 to 15 minutes. Cool on wire rack. If desired, frost with prepared vanilla frosting.   *Makes about 7 dozen cookies*

Christmas Stained Glass Cookies

Colored hard candy
¾ cup butter or margarine, softened
¾ cup granulated sugar
2 eggs
1 teaspoon vanilla extract
3 cups all-purpose flour
1 teaspoon baking powder
Frosting (optional)
Small decorative candies (optional)

Separate colors of hard candy into resealable plastic freezer bags. Crush with mallet or hammer to equal about ⅓ cup crushed candy; set aside. In mixing bowl, cream butter and sugar. Beat in eggs and vanilla. In another bowl sift together flour and baking powder. Gradually stir flour mixture into butter mixture until dough is very stiff. Wrap in plastic wrap and chill about 3 hours.

Preheat oven to 375°F. Roll out dough to ⅛-inch thickness on lightly floured surface. Additional flour may be added to dough if necessary. Cut out cookies using large Christmas cookie cutters. Transfer cookies to foil-lined baking sheet. Using small Christmas cookie cutter of the same shape as large one, cut out and remove dough from center of each cookie.* Fill cut out sections with crushed candy. If using cookies as hanging ornaments, make holes at tops of cookies for string with drinking straw or chopstick. Bake 7 to 9 minutes or until cookies are lightly browned and candy is melted. Slide foil off baking sheets. When cool, carefully loosen cookies from foil. Use frosting and candy for additional decorations, if desired.

Makes about 2½ dozen medium-sized cookies

For different designs, other cookie cutter shapes can be used to cut out center of cookies (i.e., small circle and star-shaped cutters can be used to cut out ornament designs on large Christmas tree cookies).

Favorite recipe from **The Sugar Association, Inc.**

Holiday Double Chocolate Cookies

1½ cups all-purpose flour
½ cup HERSHEY'S Cocoa
½ teaspoon baking soda
¼ teaspoon salt
½ cup (1 stick) butter or margarine, softened
¾ cup packed light brown sugar
½ cup granulated sugar
1 teaspoon vanilla extract
2 eggs
1⅓ cups (10-ounce package) HERSHEY'S Semi-Sweet Chocolate Holiday Bits, divided

1. Heat oven to 350°F. Lightly grease cookie sheet.

2. Stir together flour, cocoa, baking soda and salt. Beat butter, brown sugar, granulated sugar and vanilla in large bowl until well blended. Add eggs; beat well. Gradually add flour mixture, blending well. Stir in 1 cup bits. Drop by rounded teaspoons onto prepared cookie sheet. Press 8 to 9 of remaining bits on dough before baking.

3. Bake 7 to 9 minutes or until cookies are set. Do not overbake. Cool slightly; remove from cookie sheet to wire rack. Cool completely.

Makes about 3½ dozen cookies

Raspberry Thumbprints

1 cup less 1 tablespoon all-purpose flour (15 tablespoons)
½ teaspoon baking soda
¼ teaspoon grated lemon peel
4 tablespoons margarine (70% vegetable oil stick), softened
1 tablespoon light corn syrup
6 tablespoons sucralose-based sugar substitute*
1 teaspoon vanilla
¼ teaspoon almond extract
1 large egg white
3 tablespoons low-sugar raspberry preserves

Sold as the brand name SPLENDA®.

1. Combine flour, baking soda and lemon peel in small bowl; set aside. Beat margarine, corn syrup, sugar substitute, vanilla and almond extract in medium bowl at high speed of electric mixer until creamy. Beat in egg white. (Mixture will not cream completely.) Add flour mixture; mix well. Wrap dough in plastic wrap; refrigerate ½ hour.

2. Preheat oven to 375°F. Roll dough into 1-inch balls; place on cookie sheet. Press down center of each ball with thumb or finger to form flattened indention. Fill each center with ½ teaspoon preserves.

3. Bake 8 minutes or until firm and bottoms are lightly browned. Remove to wire rack; cool completely.

Makes 16 cookies

Pumpkin Spiced and Iced Cookies

2¼ cups all-purpose flour
1½ teaspoons pumpkin pie spice
 1 teaspoon baking powder
 ½ teaspoon baking soda
 ½ teaspoon salt
 1 cup (2 sticks) butter or margarine, softened
 1 cup granulated sugar
 1 can (15 ounces) LIBBY'S® 100% Pure Pumpkin
 2 large eggs
 1 teaspoon vanilla extract
 2 cups (12-ounce package) NESTLÉ® TOLL HOUSE® Semi-Sweet
   Chocolate Morsels
 1 cup chopped walnuts (optional)
   Vanilla Glaze (recipe follows)

PREHEAT oven to 375°F. Grease baking sheets.

COMBINE flour, pumpkin pie spice, baking powder, baking soda and salt in medium bowl. Beat butter and granulated sugar in large mixer bowl until creamy. Beat in pumpkin, eggs and vanilla extract. Gradually beat in flour mixture. Stir in morsels and nuts. Drop by rounded tablespoon onto prepared baking sheets.

BAKE for 15 to 20 minutes or until edges are lightly browned. Cool on baking sheets for 2 minutes; remove to wire rack to cool completely. Spread or drizzle with Vanilla Glaze.   *Makes about 5½ dozen cookies*

Vanilla Glaze: **COMBINE** 1 cup powdered sugar, 1 to 1½ tablespoons milk and ½ teaspoon vanilla extract in small bowl; mix well.

Cocoa Gingerbread Cookies

¼ cup (½ stick) butter, softened
2 tablespoons shortening
⅓ cup packed brown sugar
¼ cup dark molasses
1 egg
1½ cups all-purpose flour
¼ cup unsweetened cocoa powder
½ teaspoon baking soda
½ teaspoon ground ginger
½ teaspoon ground cinnamon
¼ teaspoon salt
¼ teaspoon ground nutmeg
⅛ teaspoon ground cloves
Decorator Icing (page 146)

1. Preheat oven to 400°F. Lightly grease cookie sheets or line with parchment paper. Beat butter, shortening, brown sugar and molasses in large bowl at medium speed of electric mixer. Add egg; beat until light and fluffy. Combine flour, cocoa, baking soda, ginger, cinnamon, salt, nutmeg and cloves in small bowl. Blend into creamed mixture until smooth. (If dough is too soft to handle, wrap in plastic wrap and refrigerate until firm.)

2. Roll out dough to ¼-inch thickness on lightly floured surface. Cut dough with cookie cutters. Place 2 inches apart on prepared cookie sheets. Bake 8 to 10 minutes or until firm. Remove to wire racks to cool completely. Prepare Decorator Icing. Spoon into pastry bag fitted with small tip. Decorate cookies with icing.

Makes about 6 dozen cookies

continued on page 146

Cocoa Gingerbread Cookies, continued

Decorator Icing

    1 egg white*
 3½ cups powdered sugar
    1 teaspoon almond or lemon extract
    2 to 3 tablespoons water

Use clean, uncracked egg.

Beat egg white in large bowl until frothy. Gradually beat in sugar until blended. Add almond extract and enough water to moisten. Beat until smooth and glossy.

Pistachio Cookie Cups

 ½ cup (1 stick) plus 1 tablespoon butter, softened and divided
 1 package (3 ounces) cream cheese, softened
 2 tablespoons granulated sugar
 1 cup all-purpose flour
 ½ teaspoon grated orange peel
 1 cup powdered sugar
 ½ cup chopped pistachio nuts
 ⅓ cup dried cranberries
 1 egg
 ½ teaspoon orange extract

1. Beat butter, cream cheese and granulated sugar at medium speed of electric mixer until light and fluffy. Add flour and orange peel; beat until just blended. Shape dough into ball; wrap in plastic wrap. Freeze 30 minutes.

2. Combine all remaining ingredients in small bowl; mix well. Set aside.

3. Preheat oven to 350°F. Lightly spray 24 mini muffin cups with nonstick cooking spray. Press 1 tablespoon dough firmly into bottom and up side of each muffin cup. Fill shells ¾ full with pistachio mixture.

4. Bake 25 minutes or until filling is set. Remove cookie cups to wire rack; cool completely.   *Makes 2 dozen cookies*

Cranberry Orange Ricotta Cheese Brownies

½ cup (1 stick) butter or margarine, melted
¾ cup sugar
1 teaspoon vanilla extract
2 eggs
¾ cup all-purpose flour
½ cup HERSHEY'S Cocoa
½ teaspoon baking powder
½ teaspoon salt
Cheese Filling (recipe follows)

1. Heat oven to 350°F. Grease 9-inch square baking pan.

2. Stir together butter, sugar and vanilla in medium bowl; add eggs, beating well. Stir together flour, cocoa, baking powder and salt; add to butter mixture, mixing thoroughly. Spread half of chocolate batter in prepared pan. Spread Cheese Filling over top. Drop remaining chocolate batter by teaspoonfuls onto cheese filling.

3. Bake 40 to 45 minutes or until wooden pick inserted in center comes out clean. Cool completely in pan on wire rack. Cut into squares. Refrigerate leftover brownies.

Makes about 16 brownies

Cheese Filling

1 cup ricotta cheese
¼ cup sugar
3 tablespoons whole-berry cranberry sauce
2 tablespoons cornstarch
1 egg
¼ to ½ teaspoon freshly grated orange peel
4 drops red food color (optional)

Beat ricotta cheese, sugar, cranberry sauce, cornstarch and egg in small bowl until smooth. Stir in orange peel and food color, if desired.

Festive Cakes, Pies & More

Sweet Potato Pie

Pastry for single-crust 9-inch pie
2 cups cooked, mashed sweet potatoes (about 2 pounds)
1 can (12 ounces) evaporated fat-free milk
1 cup EQUAL® SPOONFUL*
2 eggs, lightly beaten
1 tablespoon all-purpose flour
1 teaspoon lemon juice
1 teaspoon vanilla
½ teaspoon ground cinnamon
½ teaspoon ground nutmeg
½ teaspoon salt

*May substitute 24 packets Equal® sweetener.

• Roll pastry on lightly floured surface into circle 1 inch larger than inverted 9-inch pie pan. Ease pastry into pan; trim and flute edge.

• Mix sweet potatoes with electric mixer in large bowl until smooth. Stir in evaporated milk, Equal®, eggs, flour, lemon juice, vanilla, spices and salt. Pour mixture into pastry shell.

• Bake in preheated 400°F oven 40 to 45 minutes or until filling is set and sharp knife inserted in center comes out clean.

• Cool completely on wire rack. Refrigerate until serving time.   *Makes 8 servings*

Apple-Pear Praline Pie

6 cups peeled, cored and thinly sliced Granny Smith apples
3 cups peeled, cored and thinly sliced pears
¾ cup granulated sugar
¼ cup plus 1 tablespoon all-purpose flour, divided
4 tablespoons ground cinnamon
¼ teaspoon salt
  Pastry for 9-inch double crust pie
½ cup (1 stick) plus 2 tablespoons butter, divided
1 cup packed brown sugar
¼ cup half-and-half
1 cup chopped pecans

1. Preheat oven to 350°F. Combine apples, pears, granulated sugar, ¼ cup flour, cinnamon and salt in large bowl; toss gently. Let stand 15 minutes.

2. Place 1 crust in 9-inch deep dish pie pan; sprinkle lightly with remaining 1 tablespoon flour. Spoon apple and pear mixture into crust; dot with 2 tablespoons butter. Top with second pie crust. Seal and flute as desired; cut slits in crust to vent steam. Bake 50 to 55 minutes.

3. Melt remaining ½ cup butter in small saucepan over low heat. Stir in brown sugar and half-and-half. Bring to a boil, stirring constantly. Remove from heat; stir in pecans. Spread over top of pie.

4. Place pie on baking sheet; bake 5 minutes. Cool on wire rack. Serve warm or at room temperature.

Makes 8 servings

 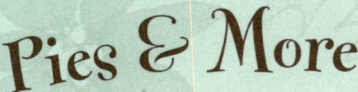
Raspberry 'N' Ginger Cream Tart

2 cups ground shortbread cookies
½ cup granulated sugar, divided
3 tablespoons very cold Butter Flavor CRISCO® Stick or 3 tablespoons very cold Butter Flavor CRISCO® Shortening
2 tablespoons milk
1½ teaspoons unflavored gelatin
⅓ cup very finely chopped crystallized ginger
1 teaspoon fresh lemon juice
⅛ teaspoon salt
2 cups heavy cream, divided
¾ cup sour cream
2 pints fresh raspberries
Confectioners' sugar

Preheat oven to 350°F.

Blend shortbread cookies, ¼ cup sugar and CRISCO® Shortening in food processor until mixture begins to clump together. Press onto bottom and up sides of a 10-inch removable bottom tart pan. Bake in the middle of the oven for about 15 minutes or until edges are lightly browned. Cool on rack.

Place 2 tablespoons milk in saucepan; sprinkle gelatin over milk and let stand 1 minute to soften. Add ginger, remaining ¼ cup sugar, lemon juice, salt and 1 cup heavy cream. Cook over moderate heat, stirring until gelatin and sugar are dissolved, about 6 to 7 minutes. Cool 1 hour. Whisk sour cream into the gelatin mixture until smooth.

Beat remaining 1 cup heavy cream in a bowl with electric mixer until soft peaks form. Gently fold gelatin mixture into heavy cream until well combined. Pour into crust and chill 8 hours or until set.

Top with fresh raspberries and a dusting of confectioners' sugar just before serving.

Makes 4 to 6 servings

Peppermint Cheesecake

Crust
- 1¼ cups vanilla wafer crumbs
- 3 tablespoons melted margarine

Filling
- 4 cups (30 ounces) SARGENTO® Light Ricotta Cheese
- ½ cup sugar
- ½ cup half-and-half
- ¼ cup all-purpose flour
- 1 teaspoon vanilla
- ¼ teaspoon salt
- 3 eggs
- 16 peppermint candies
- Fresh mint leaves (optional)

Lightly grease sides of 8- or 9-inch springform pan. Combine crumbs and margarine; mix well. Press evenly over bottom of pan. Refrigerate while preparing filling. Combine Ricotta cheese, sugar, half-and-half, flour, vanilla and salt in large bowl; beat with electric mixer until smooth. Add eggs, one at a time; beat until smooth. Place candies in heavy plastic bag. Crush with meat mallet or hammer. Reserve ¼ cup larger pieces for garnish; stir remaining crushed candies into batter. Pour batter over crust. Bake at 350°F 1 hour or until center is just set. Turn off oven; cool in oven with door propped open 30 minutes. Remove to wire cooling rack; loosen cake from rim of pan with metal spatula. Cool completely; refrigerate at least 4 hours. Immediately before serving, garnish cake around top edge with reserved crushed candies and mint leaves, if desired. *Makes 8 servings*

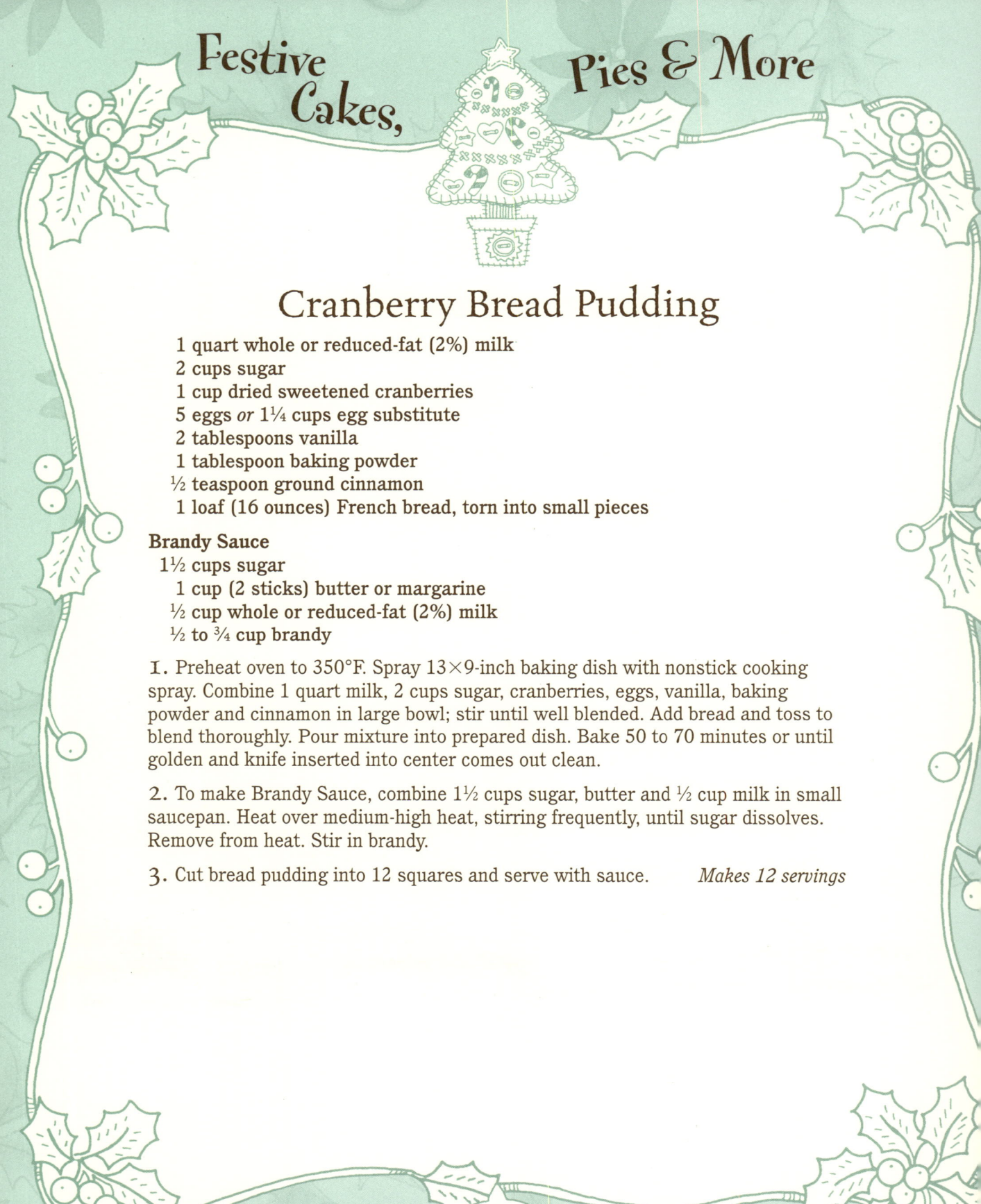

Cranberry Bread Pudding

1 quart whole or reduced-fat (2%) milk
2 cups sugar
1 cup dried sweetened cranberries
5 eggs *or* 1¼ cups egg substitute
2 tablespoons vanilla
1 tablespoon baking powder
½ teaspoon ground cinnamon
1 loaf (16 ounces) French bread, torn into small pieces

Brandy Sauce
1½ cups sugar
1 cup (2 sticks) butter or margarine
½ cup whole or reduced-fat (2%) milk
½ to ¾ cup brandy

1. Preheat oven to 350°F. Spray 13×9-inch baking dish with nonstick cooking spray. Combine 1 quart milk, 2 cups sugar, cranberries, eggs, vanilla, baking powder and cinnamon in large bowl; stir until well blended. Add bread and toss to blend thoroughly. Pour mixture into prepared dish. Bake 50 to 70 minutes or until golden and knife inserted into center comes out clean.

2. To make Brandy Sauce, combine 1½ cups sugar, butter and ½ cup milk in small saucepan. Heat over medium-high heat, stirring frequently, until sugar dissolves. Remove from heat. Stir in brandy.

3. Cut bread pudding into 12 squares and serve with sauce.   *Makes 12 servings*

Four Way Fudgey Chocolate Cake

1¼ cups all-purpose flour
1 cup sugar
1 cup nonfat milk
⅓ cup HERSHEY'S Cocoa or HERSHEY'S Dutch Processed Cocoa
⅓ cup unsweetened applesauce
1 tablespoon white vinegar
1 teaspoon baking soda
½ teaspoon vanilla extract
    Toppings (optional): Frozen light non-dairy whipped topping, thawed, REESE'S® Peanut Butter Chips, sliced strawberries, chopped almonds, raspberries

1. Heat oven to 350°F. Spray 9-inch square baking pan or 11×7×2-inch baking pan with vegetable cooking spray.

2. Stir together flour, sugar, milk, cocoa, applesauce, vinegar, baking soda and vanilla in large bowl; beat on low speed of mixer until blended. Pour batter into prepared pan.

3. Bake 30 to 35 minutes or until wooden pick inserted in center comes out clean. Cool completely in pan on wire rack.

4. Spoon whipped topping into pastry bag fitted with star tip; pipe stars in two lines to divide cake into four squares or rectangles. Using plain tip, pipe lattice design into one square; place peanut butter chips onto lattice. Place strawberries into another square. Sprinkle almonds into third square. Place raspberries into remaining square.

5. Serve immediately. Cover; refrigerate leftover cake. Store cake without toppings covered at room temperature.
Makes 12 servings

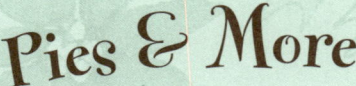
Apple Custard Tart

1 folded refrigerated unbaked pastry crust (one-half of 15-ounce package)
1 (14-ounce) can EAGLE BRAND® Sweetened Condensed Milk
   (NOT evaporated milk)
1½ cups sour cream
¼ cup thawed frozen apple juice concentrate
1 egg
1½ teaspoons vanilla extract
¼ teaspoon ground cinnamon
   Apple Cinnamon Glaze (recipe follows)
2 medium all-purpose apples, cored, pared and thinly sliced
1 tablespoon butter or margarine

1. Let refrigerated pastry crust stand at room temperature according to package directions. Preheat oven to 375°F. On floured surface, roll pastry crust from center to edge, forming circle about 13 inches in diameter. Ease pastry into 11-inch tart pan with removable bottom. Trim pastry even with rim of pan. Place pan on baking sheet. Bake crust 15 minutes or until lightly golden.

2. Meanwhile, in medium mixing bowl, beat Eagle Brand, sour cream, apple juice concentrate, egg, vanilla and cinnamon in small bowl until smooth. Pour into baked pie crust. Bake 25 minutes or until center appears set when shaken. Cool 1 hour on wire rack. Prepare Apple Cinnamon Glaze.

3. In large skillet, cook apples in butter until tender-crisp. Arrange apples on top of tart; drizzle with Apple Cinnamon Glaze. Chill in refrigerator at least 4 hours. Store leftovers loosely covered in refrigerator.   *Makes 1 tart*

Apple Cinnamon Glaze: In small saucepan, combine ⅓ cup thawed frozen apple juice concentrate, 1 teaspoon cornstarch and ½ teaspoon ground cinnamon. Mix well. Cook and stir over low heat until thick and bubbly.

Prep Time: 10 minutes
Bake Time: 40 minutes
Cool Time : 1 hour
Chill Time: 4 hours

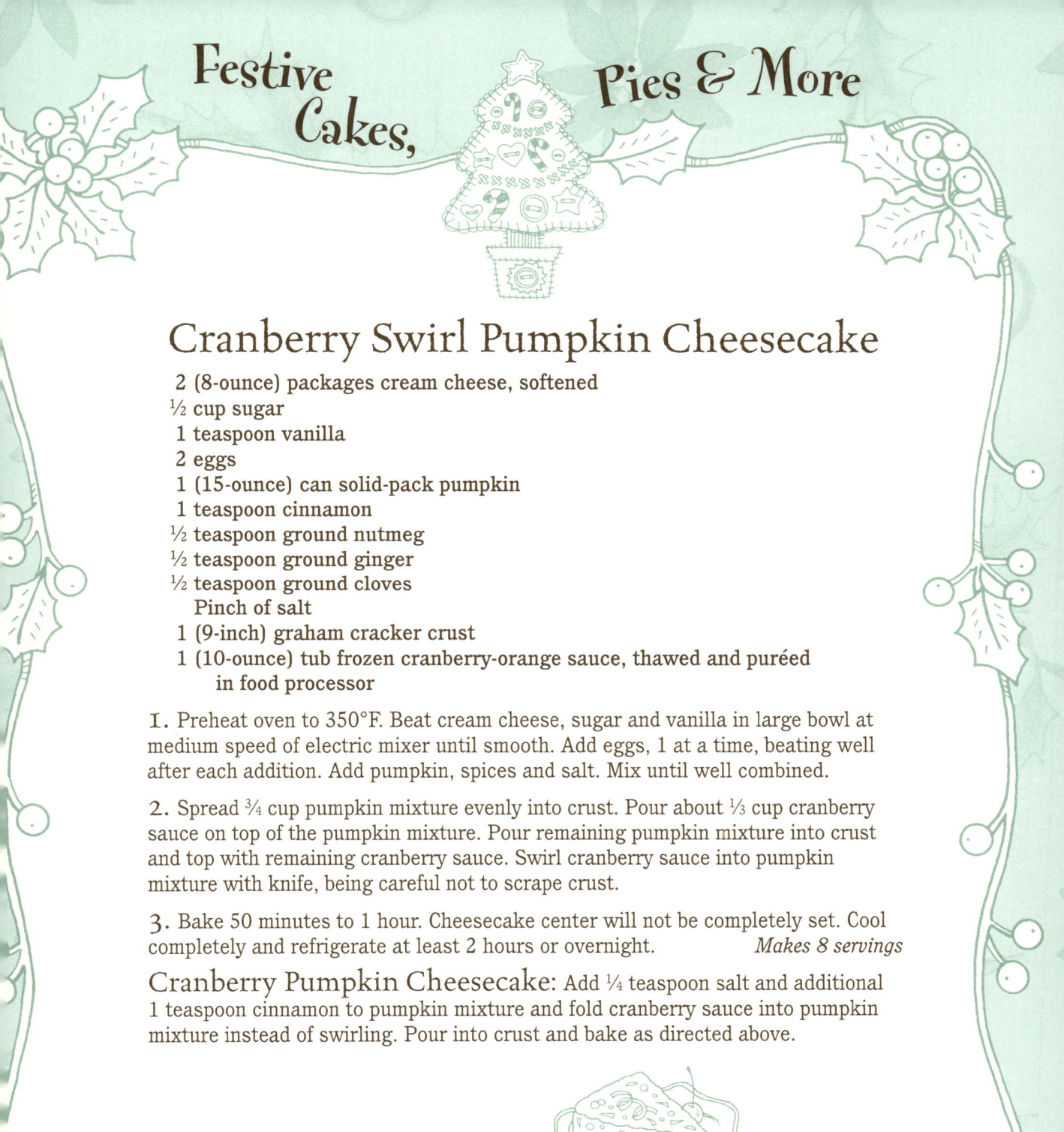

Cranberry Swirl Pumpkin Cheesecake

2 (8-ounce) packages cream cheese, softened
½ cup sugar
1 teaspoon vanilla
2 eggs
1 (15-ounce) can solid-pack pumpkin
1 teaspoon cinnamon
½ teaspoon ground nutmeg
½ teaspoon ground ginger
½ teaspoon ground cloves
Pinch of salt
1 (9-inch) graham cracker crust
1 (10-ounce) tub frozen cranberry-orange sauce, thawed and puréed
   in food processor

1. Preheat oven to 350°F. Beat cream cheese, sugar and vanilla in large bowl at medium speed of electric mixer until smooth. Add eggs, 1 at a time, beating well after each addition. Add pumpkin, spices and salt. Mix until well combined.

2. Spread ¾ cup pumpkin mixture evenly into crust. Pour about ⅓ cup cranberry sauce on top of the pumpkin mixture. Pour remaining pumpkin mixture into crust and top with remaining cranberry sauce. Swirl cranberry sauce into pumpkin mixture with knife, being careful not to scrape crust.

3. Bake 50 minutes to 1 hour. Cheesecake center will not be completely set. Cool completely and refrigerate at least 2 hours or overnight.   *Makes 8 servings*

Cranberry Pumpkin Cheesecake: Add ¼ teaspoon salt and additional 1 teaspoon cinnamon to pumpkin mixture and fold cranberry sauce into pumpkin mixture instead of swirling. Pour into crust and bake as directed above.

Ginger-Crusted Pumpkin Cheesecake

12 whole low-fat honey graham crackers, broken into small pieces
3 tablespoons reduced-fat margarine, melted
½ teaspoon ground ginger
1 can (15 ounces) solid-pack pumpkin
2 packages (8 ounces each) fat-free cream cheese, softened
1 package (8 ounces) reduced-fat cream cheese, softened
1 cup sugar
1 cup cholesterol-free egg substitute
½ cup evaporated skimmed milk
1 tablespoon vanilla
1 teaspoon ground cinnamon
½ teaspoon ground nutmeg
¼ teaspoon salt
2 cups thawed frozen reduced-fat whipped topping
    Additional ground nutmeg (optional)

1. Preheat oven to 350°F. Coat 9-inch springform pan with nonstick cooking spray; set aside.

2. Place graham crackers, margarine and ginger in food processor or blender; pulse until coarse crumbs are formed. Gently press crumb mixture onto bottom and ¾ inch up side of pan. Bake 10 minutes or until lightly browned; cool slightly on wire rack.

3. Beat remaining ingredients, except whipped topping and additional nutmeg, in large bowl at medium-high speed of electric mixer until smooth; pour into pie crust.

4. Bake 1 hour and 15 minutes or until top begins to crack and center moves very little when pan is shaken back and forth. Cool on wire rack 1 hour; refrigerate until ready to serve.

5. Just before serving, spoon 1 tablespoon whipped topping on each serving; sprinkle lightly with additional nutmeg.   *Makes 16 servings*

Note: This cheesecake freezes well. In fact, the flavors improve with freezing!

 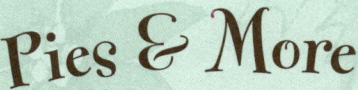
Pumpkin Carrot Cake

    2 cups all-purpose flour
    2 teaspoons baking soda
    2 teaspoons ground cinnamon
    ½ teaspoon salt
    ¾ cup milk
  1½ teaspoons lemon juice
    3 large eggs
  1¼ cups LIBBY'S® 100% Pure Pumpkin
  1½ cups granulated sugar
    ½ cup packed brown sugar
    ½ cup vegetable oil
    1 can (8 ounces) crushed pineapple, drained
    1 cup (about 3 medium) grated carrots
    1 cup flaked coconut
  1¼ cups chopped nuts, *divided*
      Cream Cheese Frosting (recipe follows)

PREHEAT oven to 350°F. Grease two 9-inch round baking pans.

COMBINE flour, baking soda, cinnamon and salt in small bowl. Combine milk and lemon juice in liquid measuring cup (mixture will appear curdled).

BEAT eggs, pumpkin, granulated sugar, brown sugar, oil, pineapple, carrots and milk mixture in large mixer bowl; mix well. Gradually add flour mixture; beat until combined. Stir in coconut and *1 cup* nuts. Pour into prepared baking pans.

BAKE for 30 to 35 minutes or until wooden pick inserted in center comes out clean. Cool in pans for 15 minutes. Remove to wire racks to cool completely.

FROST between layers, on side and top of cake with Cream Cheese Frosting. Garnish with *remaining* nuts. Store in refrigerator.   *Makes 12 servings*

Cream Cheese Frosting: **COMBINE** 11 ounces softened cream cheese,
⅓ cup softened butter and 3½ cups sifted powdered sugar in large mixer bowl until fluffy. Add 1 teaspoon vanilla extract, 2 teaspoons orange juice and 1 teaspoon grated orange peel; beat until combined.

Apple Maple Raisin Pie

Crust
2⅔ cups all-purpose flour
1 teaspoon salt
1 CRISCO® Stick or 1 cup CRISCO® all-vegetable shortening
7 to 8 tablespoons cold water

Filling
9 cups quartered, cored and peeled apples (about 2½ pounds)
½ cup raisins
¾ cup pure maple syrup (or maple-flavored pancake syrup)
¼ cup all-purpose flour
½ teaspoon salt
¼ cup heavy or whipping cream
1½ teaspoons ground cinnamon
½ teaspoon ground cardamom
Milk for brushing the crust

1. Heat the oven to 375°F.

2. For crust, combine flour and salt in medium bowl. Cut in shortening using pastry blender (or two knives) until all flour is just blended in to form pea-sized chunks. Sprinkle with water, one tablespoon at a time. Toss lightly with fork until dough forms a ball. Divide dough into two equal parts. Press between hands to form two 5- to 6-inch "pancakes."

3. Flour "pancakes" lightly on both sides. Roll one "pancake" between sheets of waxed paper (or plastic wrap) on dampened countertop for bottom crust. Peel off top sheet of waxed paper. Trim 1 inch larger than upside-down 10-inch pie plate. Flip into pie plate. Remove other sheet. Trim edge even with pie plate. Moisten edge of pastry with water.

4. For filling, toss apples and raisins in large mixing bowl with syrup, flour, salt, cream, cinnamon and cardamom. Mound filling in the pie shell.

5. Roll top crust same as bottom using second "pancake" to ⅛-inch thick. Peel off top sheet of waxed paper. Flip onto filled pie. Remove other sheet of waxed paper. Trim ½ inch beyond edge of pie plate. Fold top edge under bottom crust. Flute. Brush crust with milk. Cut slits in top crust for escape of steam.

6. Bake at 375°F for 1¼ to 1½ hours, or until crust is golden brown and filling is bubbling. DO NOT OVERBAKE. Cover pie loosely with foil to prevent over-browning, if necessary. Cool at least 1 hour before serving. *Makes 1 (10-inch) pie*

Spiced Gingerbread

1½ cups bran flakes
1 cup milk
1½ cups all-purpose flour
2 teaspoons baking soda
1 teaspoon ground cinnamon
1 teaspoon ground ginger
½ teaspoon ground cloves
1 cup GRANDMA'S® Molasses
½ cup butter, melted
3 eggs
Confectioners' sugar (optional)

1. Heat oven to 350°F. In large bowl, mix bran flakes and milk; let stand 5 minutes. In separate bowl, mix flour, baking soda, cinnamon, ginger and cloves; set aside. In another bowl, with electric mixer at medium speed, beat molasses, butter and eggs until smooth. Blend in bran and flour mixtures. Pour batter into greased and floured 13×9×2-inch baking pan.

2. Bake 40 to 45 minutes or until toothpick inserted in center comes out clean. Cool in pan 10 minutes. Remove from pan; cool completely on wire rack. Sprinkle with confectioners' sugar if desired; cut into 2½×2-inch pieces to serve.
Makes 20 servings

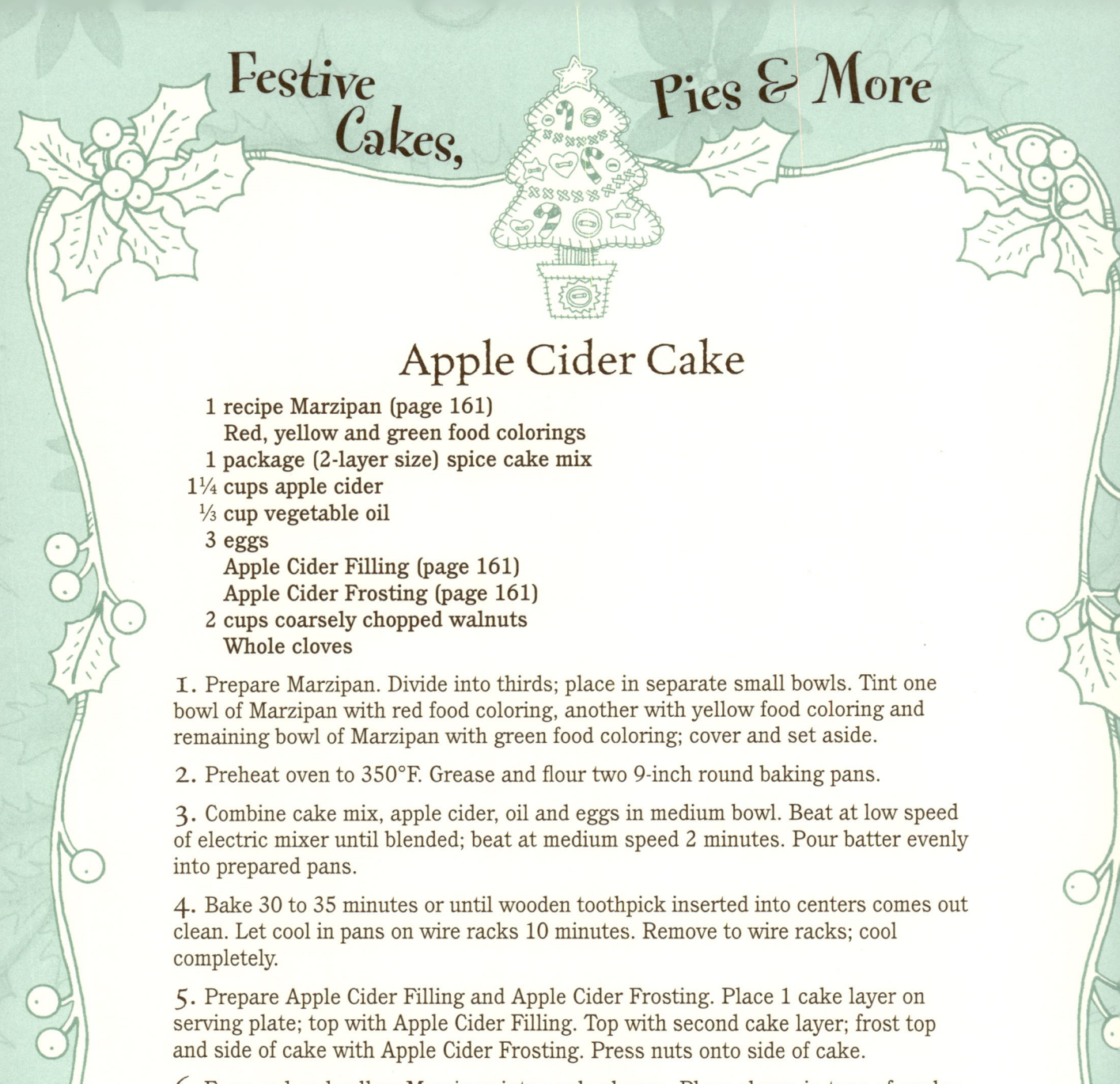

Apple Cider Cake

1 recipe Marzipan (page 161)
   Red, yellow and green food colorings
1 package (2-layer size) spice cake mix
1¼ cups apple cider
⅓ cup vegetable oil
3 eggs
   Apple Cider Filling (page 161)
   Apple Cider Frosting (page 161)
2 cups coarsely chopped walnuts
   Whole cloves

1. Prepare Marzipan. Divide into thirds; place in separate small bowls. Tint one bowl of Marzipan with red food coloring, another with yellow food coloring and remaining bowl of Marzipan with green food coloring; cover and set aside.

2. Preheat oven to 350°F. Grease and flour two 9-inch round baking pans.

3. Combine cake mix, apple cider, oil and eggs in medium bowl. Beat at low speed of electric mixer until blended; beat at medium speed 2 minutes. Pour batter evenly into prepared pans.

4. Bake 30 to 35 minutes or until wooden toothpick inserted into centers comes out clean. Let cool in pans on wire racks 10 minutes. Remove to wire racks; cool completely.

5. Prepare Apple Cider Filling and Apple Cider Frosting. Place 1 cake layer on serving plate; top with Apple Cider Filling. Top with second cake layer; frost top and side of cake with Apple Cider Frosting. Press nuts onto side of cake.

6. Form red and yellow Marzipan into apple shapes. Place cloves in tops of apples for stems. Roll out green Marzipan to ¼-inch thickness; cut out leaf shapes as desired. Arrange on top and around side of cake.   *Makes 12 servings*

Marzipan

1 can (8 ounces) almond paste
1 egg white*
3 cups powdered sugar

Use only grade A clean, uncracked egg.

Combine almond paste and egg white in small bowl. Add 2 cups powdered sugar; mix well. Knead in remaining 1 cup sugar until smooth and pliable. Wrap tightly in plastic wrap; refrigerate until ready to use.   *Makes about 2 cups*

Apple Cider Filling

⅓ cup sugar
3 tablespoons cornstarch
⅔ cup apple cider
½ cup apple butter
2 tablespoons lemon juice
2 tablespoons butter or margarine

Combine sugar and cornstarch in small saucepan. Stir in cider and apple butter; cook over medium heat, stirring constantly, until thickened. Remove from heat; stir in lemon juice and butter. Cool completely.   *Makes about 1¼ cups*

Apple Cider Frosting

½ cup (1 stick) butter or margarine, softened
¼ cup apple cider
4 cups (about 1 pound) powdered sugar

Beat butter and cider in medium bowl at medium speed of electric mixer until creamy and well blended. Gradually beat in powdered sugar until smooth.
    Makes about 4 cups

 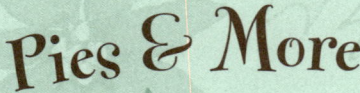
Glazed Cranberry Mini-Cakes

⅓ cup butter or margarine, softened
⅓ cup granulated sugar
⅓ cup packed light brown sugar
 1 egg
1¼ teaspoons vanilla extract
1⅓ cups all-purpose flour
 ¾ teaspoon baking powder
 ¼ teaspoon baking soda
 ¼ teaspoon salt
 2 tablespoons milk
1¼ cups coarsely chopped fresh cranberries
 ½ cup coarsely chopped walnuts
1⅔ cups HERSHEY'S Premier White Chips, divided
    White Glaze (recipe follows)

1. Heat oven to 350°F. Lightly grease or paper-line small muffin cups (1¾ inches in diameter).

2. Beat butter, granulated sugar, brown sugar, egg and vanilla in large bowl until fluffy. Stir together flour, baking powder, baking soda and salt; gradually blend into butter mixture. Add milk; stir until blended. Stir in cranberries, walnuts and ⅔ cup white chips (reserve remaining chips for glaze). Fill muffin cups almost full with batter.

3. Bake 18 to 20 minutes or until wooden pick inserted in center comes out clean. Cool 5 minutes; remove from pans to wire rack. Cool completely. Prepare White Glaze; drizzle over top of mini-cakes. Refrigerate 10 minutes to set glaze.

Makes about 3 dozen mini-cakes

White Glaze: Place remaining 1 cup HERSHEY'S Premier White Chips in small microwave-safe bowl; sprinkle 2 tablespoons vegetable oil over chips. Microwave at HIGH (100% power) 30 seconds; stir. If necessary, microwave at HIGH additional 30 seconds or just until chips are melted when stirred.

Oats 'n' Apple Tart

1½ cups uncooked quick oats
½ cup brown sugar, divided
1 tablespoon plus ¼ teaspoon ground cinnamon, divided
5 tablespoons butter or margarine, melted
2 medium sweet apples, such as Golden Delicious, unpeeled,
   cored and thinly sliced
1 teaspoon lemon juice
¼ cup water
1 envelope unsweetened gelatin
½ cup apple juice concentrate
1 package (8 ounces) reduced-fat cream cheese, softened
⅛ teaspoon ground nutmeg

1. Preheat oven to 350°F. Combine oats, ¼ cup brown sugar and 1 tablespoon cinnamon in medium bowl. Add butter and stir until combined. Press onto bottom and up side of 9-inch pie plate. Bake 7 minutes or until set. Cool on wire rack.

2. Toss apple slices with lemon juice in small bowl; set aside. Place water in small saucepan. Sprinkle gelatin over water; let stand 3 to 5 minutes. Stir in apple juice concentrate. Cook and stir over medium heat until gelatin is dissolved. *Do not boil.* Remove from heat and set aside.

3. Beat cream cheese at medium speed of electric mixer in medium bowl until fluffy and smooth. Add remaining ¼ cup brown sugar, ¼ teaspoon cinnamon and nutmeg. Mix until smooth. Slowly beat in gelatin mixture on low speed until blended and creamy, about 1 minute. *Do not overbeat.*

4. Arrange apple slices in crust. Pour cream cheese mixture evenly over top. Refrigerate 2 hours or until set. Garnish if desired.   *Makes 8 servings*

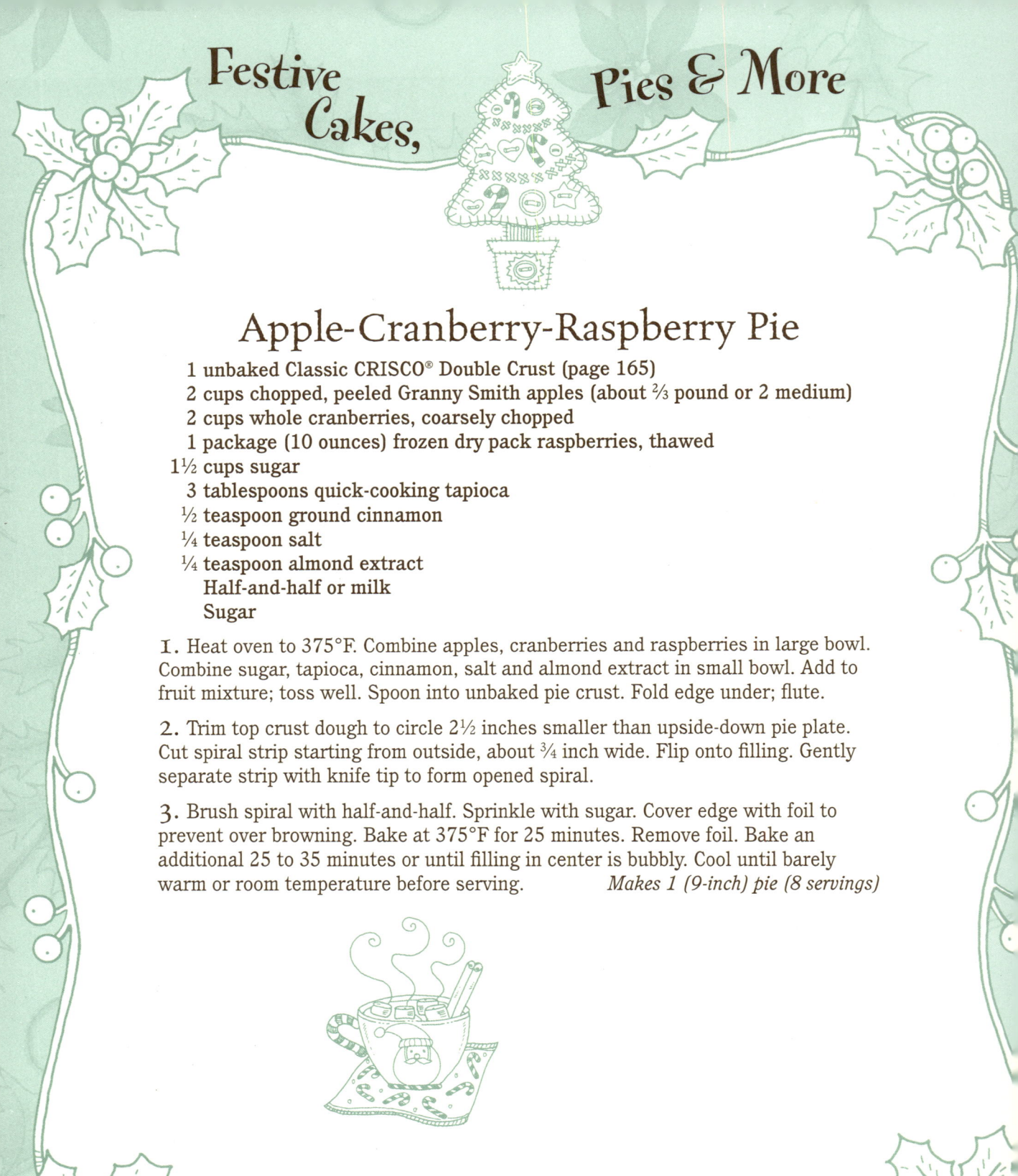

Apple-Cranberry-Raspberry Pie

1 unbaked Classic CRISCO® Double Crust (page 165)
2 cups chopped, peeled Granny Smith apples (about ⅔ pound or 2 medium)
2 cups whole cranberries, coarsely chopped
1 package (10 ounces) frozen dry pack raspberries, thawed
1½ cups sugar
3 tablespoons quick-cooking tapioca
½ teaspoon ground cinnamon
¼ teaspoon salt
¼ teaspoon almond extract
    Half-and-half or milk
    Sugar

1. Heat oven to 375°F. Combine apples, cranberries and raspberries in large bowl. Combine sugar, tapioca, cinnamon, salt and almond extract in small bowl. Add to fruit mixture; toss well. Spoon into unbaked pie crust. Fold edge under; flute.

2. Trim top crust dough to circle 2½ inches smaller than upside-down pie plate. Cut spiral strip starting from outside, about ¾ inch wide. Flip onto filling. Gently separate strip with knife tip to form opened spiral.

3. Brush spiral with half-and-half. Sprinkle with sugar. Cover edge with foil to prevent over browning. Bake at 375°F for 25 minutes. Remove foil. Bake an additional 25 to 35 minutes or until filling in center is bubbly. Cool until barely warm or room temperature before serving.   *Makes 1 (9-inch) pie (8 servings)*

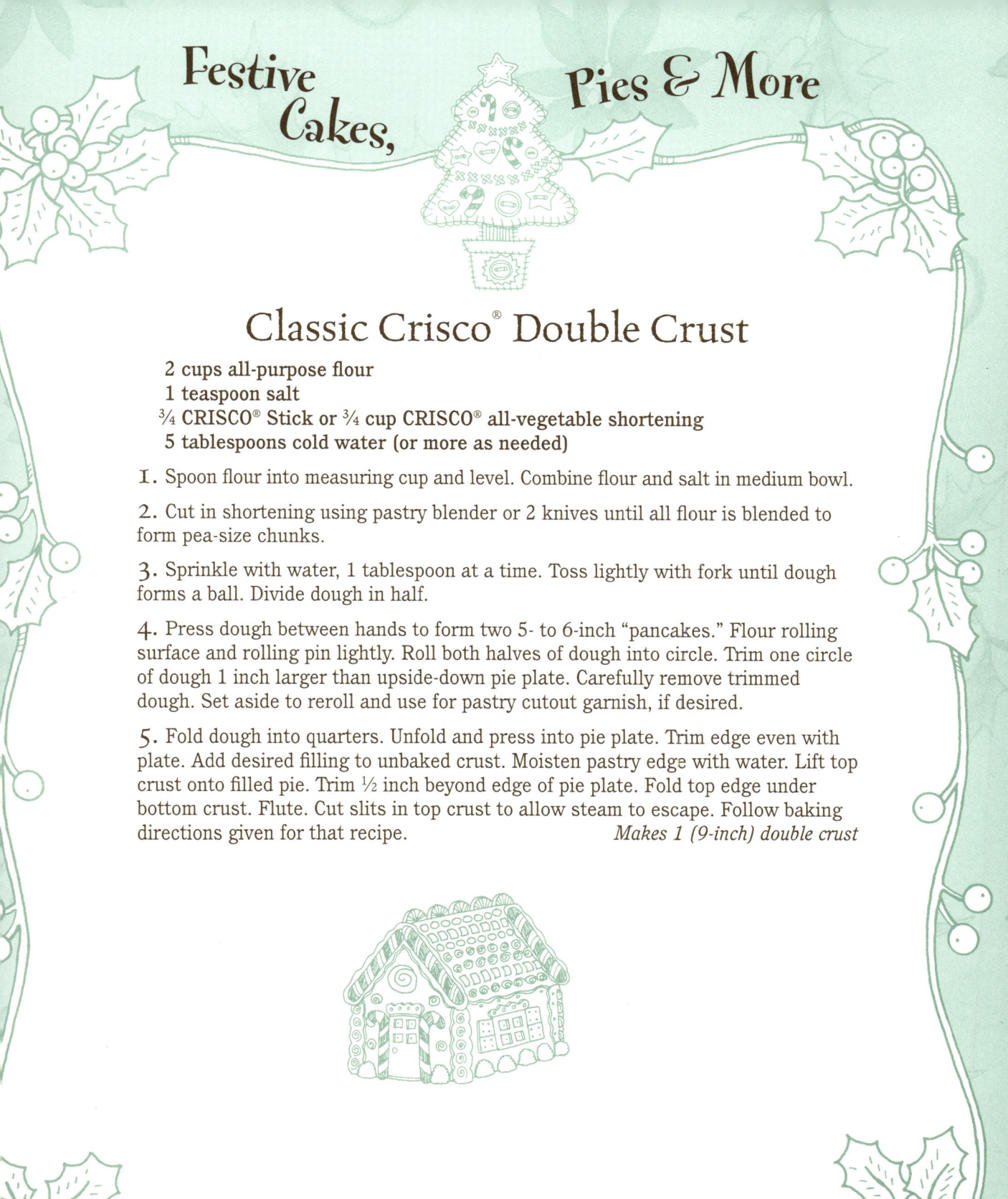

Classic Crisco® Double Crust

2 cups all-purpose flour
1 teaspoon salt
¾ CRISCO® Stick or ¾ cup CRISCO® all-vegetable shortening
5 tablespoons cold water (or more as needed)

1. Spoon flour into measuring cup and level. Combine flour and salt in medium bowl.

2. Cut in shortening using pastry blender or 2 knives until all flour is blended to form pea-size chunks.

3. Sprinkle with water, 1 tablespoon at a time. Toss lightly with fork until dough forms a ball. Divide dough in half.

4. Press dough between hands to form two 5- to 6-inch "pancakes." Flour rolling surface and rolling pin lightly. Roll both halves of dough into circle. Trim one circle of dough 1 inch larger than upside-down pie plate. Carefully remove trimmed dough. Set aside to reroll and use for pastry cutout garnish, if desired.

5. Fold dough into quarters. Unfold and press into pie plate. Trim edge even with plate. Add desired filling to unbaked crust. Moisten pastry edge with water. Lift top crust onto filled pie. Trim ½ inch beyond edge of pie plate. Fold top edge under bottom crust. Flute. Cut slits in top crust to allow steam to escape. Follow baking directions given for that recipe. *Makes 1 (9-inch) double crust*

Pumpkin Pecan Pie

1 can (15 ounces) solid-pack pumpkin
1 can (14 ounces) sweetened condensed milk
¼ cup (½ stick) butter, softened
2 eggs, divided
1 teaspoon ground cinnamon
1 teaspoon vanilla
½ teaspoon ground nutmeg
¼ teaspoon salt
1 graham cracker crust (9 inches)
2 tablespoons packed brown sugar
2 tablespoons dark corn syrup
1 tablespoon butter, melted
½ teaspoon maple flavoring
1 cup chopped pecans

1. Preheat oven to 400°F.

2. Combine pumpkin, condensed milk, softened butter, 1 egg, cinnamon, vanilla, nutmeg and salt in large bowl. Pour into pie crust. Bake 20 minutes.

3. Beat remaining egg, brown sugar, corn syrup, melted butter and maple flavoring in medium bowl at medium speed of electric mixer until well blended. Stir in pecans.

4. Remove pie from oven; top with pecan mixture. *Reduce oven temperature to 350°F.* Bake 25 minutes more or until knife inserted near center comes out clean.

Makes 8 to 10 servings

Easy Egg Nog Pound Cake

1 (18.25-ounce) package yellow cake mix
1 (4-serving size) package instant vanilla pudding and pie filling mix
¾ cup BORDEN® Egg Nog
¾ cup vegetable oil
4 eggs
½ teaspoon ground nutmeg
Powdered sugar, if desired

1. Preheat oven to 350°F. In large mixing bowl, combine cake mix, pudding mix, Borden Egg Nog and oil; beat at low speed of electric mixer until moistened. Add eggs and nutmeg; beat at medium-high speed 4 minutes.

2. Pour into greased and floured 10-inch fluted or tube pan.

3. Bake 40 to 45 minutes or until wooden pick inserted near center comes out clean.

4. Cool 10 minutes; remove from pan. Cool completely. Sprinkle with powdered sugar, if desired.   *Makes 1 (10-inch) cake*

Prep Time : 10 minutes
Bake Time: 40 to 45 minutes

Spicy Gingerbread with Cinnamon Pear Sauce

  2 cups all-purpose flour
  1 cup light molasses
  ¾ cup buttermilk
  ½ cup (1 stick) butter, softened
  ½ cup packed light brown sugar
  1 teaspoon baking soda
  1 teaspoon ground ginger
  1 teaspoon ground cinnamon
  ¼ teaspoon ground cloves
  ¼ teaspoon salt
     Cinnamon Pear Sauce (recipe follows)

1. Preheat oven to 325°F. Grease and lightly flour 9-inch square baking pan.

2. Combine all ingredients except Cinnamon Pear Sauce in large bowl. Beat at low speed of electric mixer until well blended, scraping side of bowl with rubber spatula frequently. Beat at high speed 2 minutes more. Pour into prepared pan.

3. Bake 50 to 55 minutes or until wooden toothpick inserted into center comes out clean. Cool in pan on wire rack about 30 minutes. Prepare Cinnamon Pear Sauce. Cut into squares; serve warm with sauce.   *Makes 9 servings*

Cinnamon Pear Sauce

  2 cans (16 ounces each) pear halves in syrup, undrained
  2 tablespoons granulated sugar
  1 teaspoon fresh lemon juice
  ½ teaspoon ground cinnamon

Drain pear halves, reserving ¼ cup syrup. Place pears, reserved syrup, granulated sugar, lemon juice and cinnamon in bowl of food processor or blender; cover. Process until smooth. Serve warm.   *Makes 2 cups sauce*

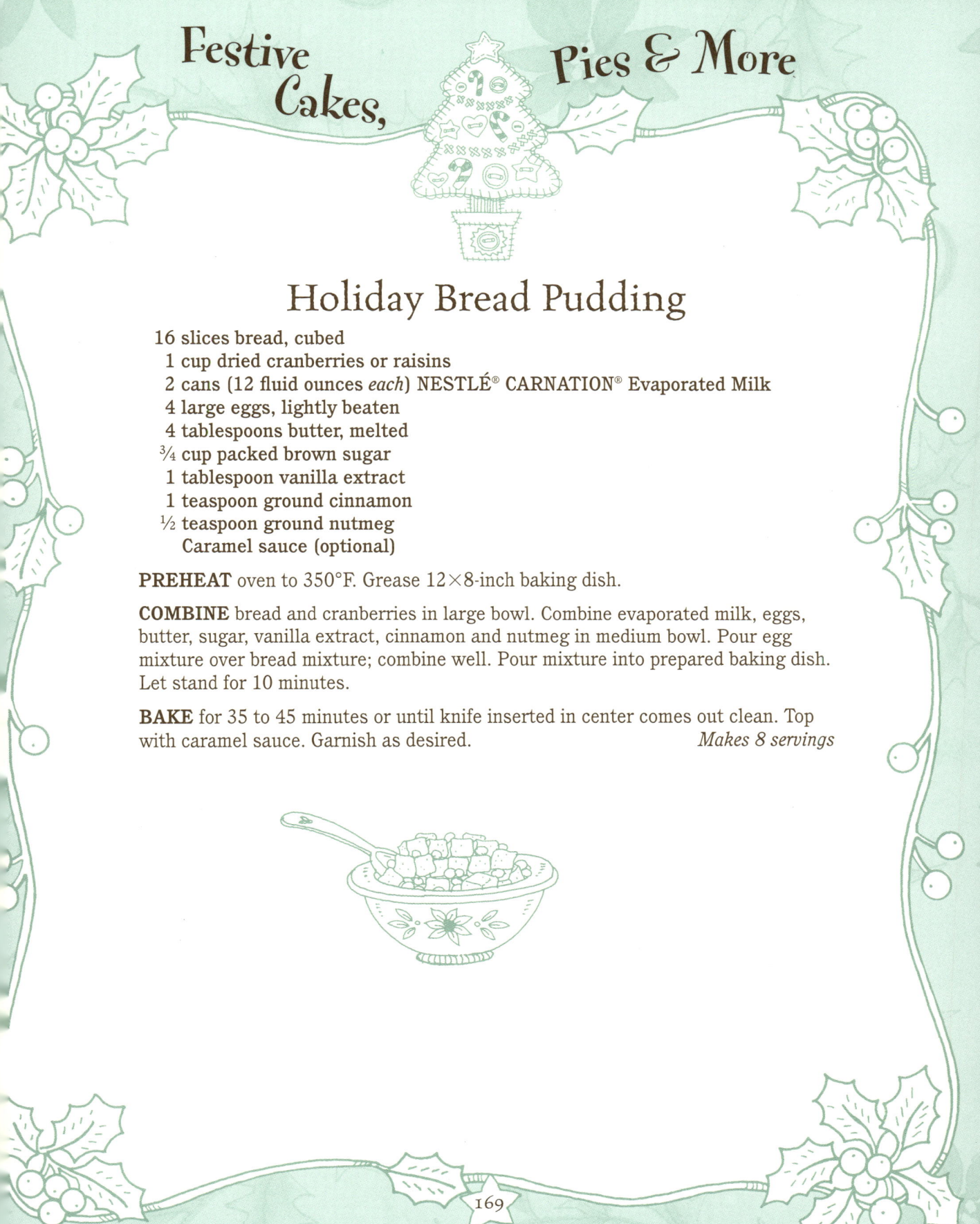

Holiday Bread Pudding

16 slices bread, cubed
1 cup dried cranberries or raisins
2 cans (12 fluid ounces *each*) NESTLÉ® CARNATION® Evaporated Milk
4 large eggs, lightly beaten
4 tablespoons butter, melted
¾ cup packed brown sugar
1 tablespoon vanilla extract
1 teaspoon ground cinnamon
½ teaspoon ground nutmeg
Caramel sauce (optional)

PREHEAT oven to 350°F. Grease 12×8-inch baking dish.

COMBINE bread and cranberries in large bowl. Combine evaporated milk, eggs, butter, sugar, vanilla extract, cinnamon and nutmeg in medium bowl. Pour egg mixture over bread mixture; combine well. Pour mixture into prepared baking dish. Let stand for 10 minutes.

BAKE for 35 to 45 minutes or until knife inserted in center comes out clean. Top with caramel sauce. Garnish as desired. *Makes 8 servings*

Chocolate Raspberry Cake

4 (1-ounce) squares unsweetened chocolate
¼ cup water
½ cup butter or margarine, cut into small pieces
½ cup sugar
3 eggs, separated
⅓ cup all-purpose flour
½ cup SMUCKER'S® Red Raspberry Preserves or Apricot Preserves
   Chocolate shavings
   Fresh raspberries

Preheat oven to 325°F. Grease and flour 2 (8-inch) round cake pans; set aside.

In a medium saucepan, melt chocolate and water over low heat, stirring constantly. Add butter; stir until completely melted. Remove from heat and blend in sugar; cool.

Add egg yolks, beating well after each addition. Add flour to chocolate mixture; blend well. Beat egg whites until stiff but not dry; fold into chocolate mixture. Pour into prepared cake pans.

Bake for 25 minutes or until toothpick inserted into center of cake comes out clean. Remove cakes from pans and cool completely on wire rack.

Heat SMUCKER'S® preserves in saucepan until melted. Spread half of preserves on 1 layer. Top with second layer; spread with remaining preserves. Garnish with chocolate shavings and raspberries.   *Makes 12 to 15 servings*

Tip: For chocolate shavings, melt 1 to 2 ounces of semisweet chocolate. Spread melted chocolate in thick layer on cookie sheet; refrigerate until set. Scrape with metal spatula held at 45° angle to produce shavings and curls. Chill or freeze shavings until ready to use.

Decadent Holiday Chocolate Torte

    3 eggs, separated
⅛ teaspoon cream of tartar
1½ cups sugar
    1 cup (2 sticks) butter or margarine, melted
    2 teaspoons vanilla extract
½ cup all-purpose flour
½ cup HERSHEY'S Cocoa or HERSHEY'S Dutch Processed Cocoa
¼ cup water
    1 cup finely chopped pecans
      Semi-Sweet Glaze (recipe follows)
      Snowy White Cut-Outs (optional)
      HERSHEY'S Holiday Bits (optional)

1. Heat oven to 350°F. Line bottom and sides of 9-inch springform pan with foil; grease foil.

2. Beat egg whites and cream of tartar in small bowl until soft peaks form; set aside. Beat egg yolks, sugar, melted butter and vanilla in large bowl until well blended. Add flour, cocoa and water; stir in pecans. Gradually fold reserved egg white mixture into chocolate mixture; spread into prepared pan.

3. Bake 45 to 55 minutes or until firm to touch; cool completely in pan on wire rack. Invert onto serving plate; remove foil. Cover; refrigerate. Prepare Semi-Sweet Glaze. Spread top and sides of torte with prepared glaze. Cover; refrigerate. Prepare Snowy White Cut-Outs, if desired; garnish top of torte with cut-outs. Press holiday bits onto sides, if desired.   *Makes 12 servings*

Semi-Sweet Glaze: Place 1 cup HERSHEY'S Semi-Sweet Chocolate Chips and ⅓ cup whipping cream in small microwave-safe bowl. Microwave at HIGH (100%) 1 minute; stir until smooth. Use immediately.

Snowy White Cut-Outs: Line tray with heavy duty foil. Melt 1⅔ cups (10-ounce package) HERSHEY'S Premier White Chips and 1 teaspoon shortening (do not use butter, margarine, spread or oil) as directed on package. Immediately spread mixture about ⅛-inch thick on prepared tray. Before mixture is firm, cut into desired shapes with small cookie cutters; do not remove from tray. Cover; refrigerate until firm. Gently peel off shapes.

My Best Apple Pie

Crust
- 1 cup all-purpose flour
- 1 cup whole wheat flour
- 1 teaspoon salt
- ½ teaspoon cinnamon
- ¾ CRISCO® Stick or ¾ cup CRISCO® all-vegetable shortening
- 5 tablespoons cold water

Filling
- 4 cups sliced, peeled (¼-inch slices) Golden Delicious apples (about 1⅓ pounds or 4 medium)
- 3 cups sliced, peeled (¼-inch slices) Granny Smith apples (about 1 pound or 3 medium)
- ¼ cup apple juice
- 2 tablespoons lemon juice
- ½ cup granulated sugar
- ½ cup firmly packed light brown sugar
- ¾ teaspoon cinnamon
- ½ teaspoon nutmeg
- 2 tablespoons plus 1½ teaspoons quick-cooking tapioca
- 1 teaspoon vanilla

1. For crust, combine all-purpose flour, whole wheat flour, salt and ½ teaspoon cinnamon in large bowl. See page 165 (Classic Crisco® Double Crust) for remaining preparation. Roll and press bottom crust into 9-inch pie plate. Cover. Do not bake.

2. For filling, combine apples, apple juice and lemon juice in large saucepan. Cook and stir on high heat 5 minutes or until apples are slightly tender. Pour into large shallow dish. Place in refrigerator, uncovered, until cool, about 20 minutes.

3. Heat oven to 400°F.

4. Spoon apples and any liquid into large bowl. Add granulated sugar, brown sugar, ¾ teaspoon cinnamon, nutmeg, tapioca and vanilla. Toss to coat. Spoon into unbaked pie crust. Moisten pastry edge with water.

5. Lift top crust onto filled pie. Trim ½ inch beyond edge of pie plate. Fold top edge under bottom crust. Flute. Cut slits in top crust to allow steam to escape.

6. Bake at 400°F for 15 minutes. Reduce oven temperature to 350°F. Bake 1 hour or until filling in center is bubbly and crust is golden brown. *Do not overbake.* Cool to room temperature before serving.   *Makes 1 (9-inch) pie*

Date Gingerbread

1¼ cups plus 1 teaspoon all-purpose flour, divided
¾ cup finely chopped pitted dates (about 18 whole dates)
½ cup whole wheat flour
¼ cup packed brown sugar
1 tablespoon (½ ounce) finely chopped candied ginger
½ teaspoon baking powder
½ teaspoon baking soda
½ teaspoon ground ginger
½ teaspoon ground nutmeg
½ cup water
½ cup molasses
¼ cup canola or vegetable oil
2 egg whites
Orange slices, for garnish

1. Preheat oven to 350°F. Coat 8-inch round baking pan with nonstick cooking spray. Dust with 1 teaspoon all-purpose flour; set aside.

2. Combine remaining 1¼ cups all-purpose flour, dates, whole wheat flour, sugar, candied ginger, baking powder, baking soda, ground ginger and nutmeg in large bowl. Add water, molasses, oil and egg whites. Beat at low speed of electric mixer until combined. Increase speed to high; beat 2 minutes. Pour into prepared pan.

3. Bake 38 to 40 minutes or until wooden toothpick inserted into center comes out clean. Cool in pan on wire rack 10 minutes. Cut into wedges and serve warm. Garnish with orange slices.   *Makes 8 servings*

Festive Cakes, Pies & More

Mott's® Peppermint Cake

Cake
- 2¼ cups cake flour
- 2 teaspoons baking powder
- 1 teaspoon salt
- ½ teaspoon baking soda
- 1½ cups sugar
- 2 tablespoons margarine
- ½ cup MOTT'S® Natural Apple Sauce
- ½ cup skim milk
- 4 egg whites
- 1 teaspoon vanilla extract

Peppermint Frosting
- 1½ cups sugar
- ¼ cup water
- 2 egg whites
- ¼ teaspoon cream of tartar
- ½ teaspoon peppermint extract
- 4 peppermint-flavored hard candies, crushed

1. Preheat oven to 375°F. Spray 9-inch round cake pan with nonstick cooking spray.

2. To prepare Cake, in medium bowl, combine flour, baking powder, salt and baking soda. In large bowl, beat 1½ cups sugar and margarine with electric mixer at medium speed until blended. Whisk in apple sauce, milk, 4 egg whites and vanilla extract.

3. Add flour mixture to apple sauce mixture; stir until well blended. Pour into prepared cake pan.

4. Bake 35 to 40 minutes or until toothpick inserted in center comes out clean. Cool completely on wire rack. Split cake horizontally in half to make 2 layers.

5. To prepare Peppermint Frosting, in top of double boiler, whisk together 1½ cups sugar, water, 2 egg whites and cream of tartar. Cook, whisking occasionally, over simmering water 4 minutes or until mixture is hot and sugar is dissolved. Remove

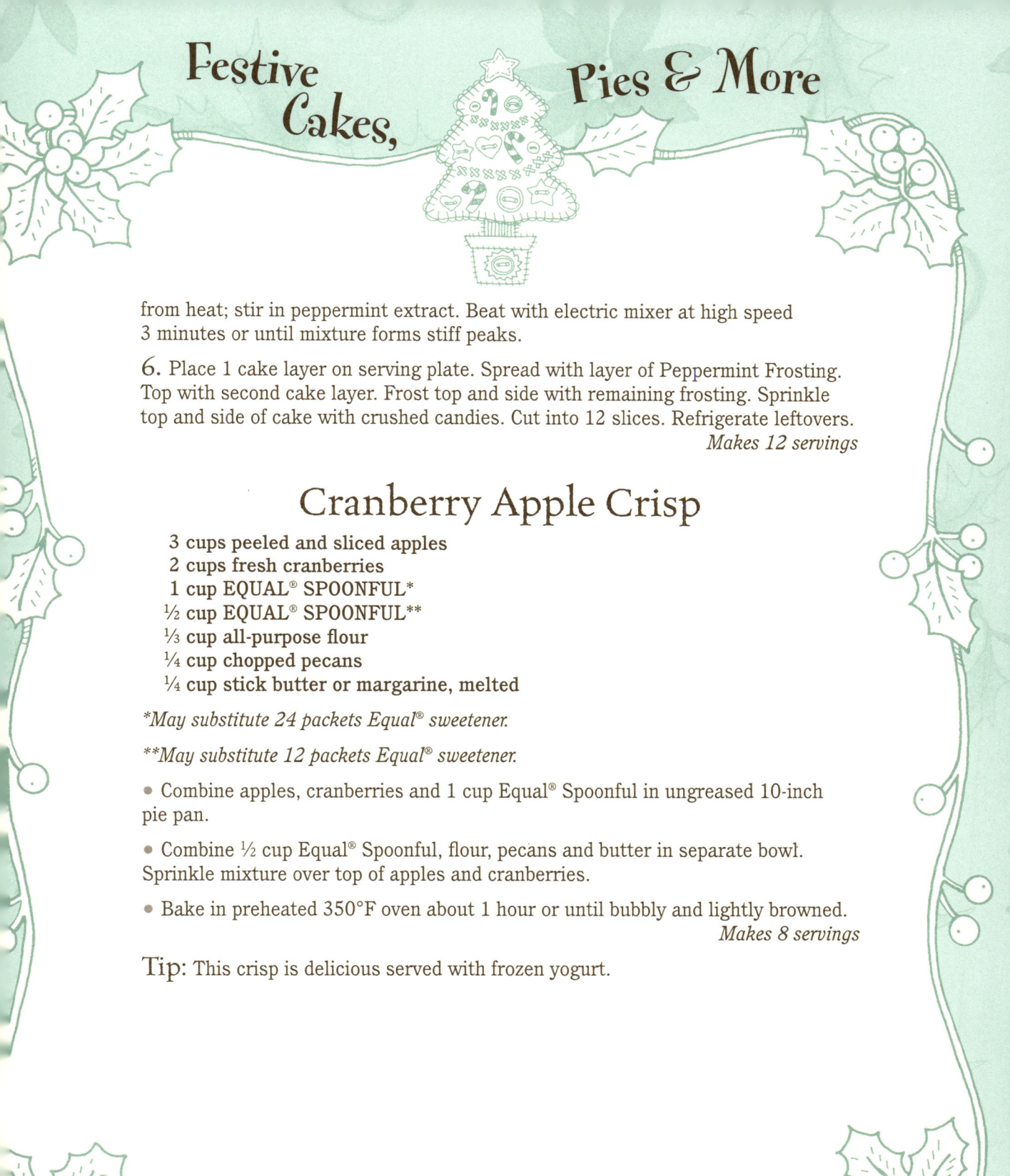

from heat; stir in peppermint extract. Beat with electric mixer at high speed 3 minutes or until mixture forms stiff peaks.

6. Place 1 cake layer on serving plate. Spread with layer of Peppermint Frosting. Top with second cake layer. Frost top and side with remaining frosting. Sprinkle top and side of cake with crushed candies. Cut into 12 slices. Refrigerate leftovers.

Makes 12 servings

Cranberry Apple Crisp

    3 cups peeled and sliced apples
    2 cups fresh cranberries
    1 cup EQUAL® SPOONFUL*
    ½ cup EQUAL® SPOONFUL**
    ⅓ cup all-purpose flour
    ¼ cup chopped pecans
    ¼ cup stick butter or margarine, melted

May substitute 24 packets Equal® sweetener.

**May substitute 12 packets Equal® sweetener.*

• Combine apples, cranberries and 1 cup Equal® Spoonful in ungreased 10-inch pie pan.

• Combine ½ cup Equal® Spoonful, flour, pecans and butter in separate bowl. Sprinkle mixture over top of apples and cranberries.

• Bake in preheated 350°F oven about 1 hour or until bubbly and lightly browned.

Makes 8 servings

Tip: This crisp is delicious served with frozen yogurt.

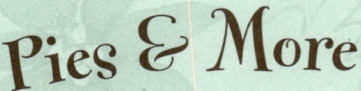
Praline Pumpkin Tart

1¼ cups all-purpose flour
  1 tablespoon granulated sugar
¾ teaspoon salt, divided
¼ cup vegetable shortening
¼ cup (½ stick) butter
  3 to 4 tablespoons cold water
  1 can (15 ounces) solid-pack pumpkin
  1 can (12 ounces) evaporated milk
⅔ cup packed brown sugar
  2 eggs
  1 teaspoon ground cinnamon
½ teaspoon ground ginger
¼ teaspoon ground cloves
    Praline Topping (page 177)
    Sweetened Whipped Cream (page 177)
    Additional cinnamon and pecans halves for garnish

1. For crust, combine flour, granulated sugar and ¼ teaspoon salt in large bowl. Cut in shortening and butter using pastry blender or 2 knives until mixture forms pea-sized pieces.

2. Sprinkle flour mixture with water, 1 tablespoon at a time. Toss with fork until mixture holds together. Shape into ball. Wrap in plastic wrap. Refrigerate about 1 hour or until chilled.

3. Roll out dough on lightly floured surface into circle 1 inch larger than inverted 10-inch tart pan with removable bottom or 1½ inches larger than inverted 9-inch pie plate. Transfer dough to tart pan or pie plate; cover with plastic wrap and refrigerate 30 minutes.

4. Preheat oven to 400°F. Pierce crust with tines of fork at ¼-inch intervals. Line tart pan with foil; fill with dried beans, uncooked rice or ceramic pie weights.

5. Bake 10 minutes or until set. Remove from oven; gently remove foil lining and beans. Return to oven and bake 5 minutes or until very light brown. Cool completely on wire rack.

6. For filling, beat pumpkin, milk, brown sugar, eggs, cinnamon, remaining ½ teaspoon salt, ginger and cloves in large bowl at low speed of electric mixer. Pour into cooled tart crust. Bake 35 minutes.

7. Prepare Praline Topping. Sprinkle topping over center of tart, leaving 1½-inch rim around edge of tart. Bake 15 minutes more or until knife inserted 1 inch from center comes out clean.

8. Cool completely on wire rack. Prepare Sweetened Whipped Cream and pipe decoratively around edge of pie. Sprinkle additional cinnamon over whipped cream. Garnish with pecan halves.   *Makes 8 servings*

Praline Topping

⅓ **cup packed brown sugar**
⅓ **cup chopped pecans**
⅓ **cup uncooked quick oats**
1 **tablespoon butter or margarine, softened**

Place sugar, pecans and oats in small bowl. Cut in butter with pastry blender or 2 knives until crumbs form.

Sweetened Whipped Cream

1 **cup heavy cream**
2 **tablespoons powdered sugar**
½ **teaspoon vanilla**

Chill large bowl, beaters and cream before whipping. Place cream, sugar and vanilla into chilled bowl and beat with electric mixer at high speed until soft peaks form. *Do not overbeat.* Refrigerate until ready to serve.   *Makes about 2 cups*

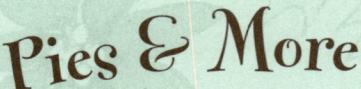
Bittersweet Chocolate Torte

Torte
- 6 tablespoons stick butter or margarine
- 4 ounces unsweetened chocolate
- ⅓ cup fat-free milk
- ⅓ cup sugar-free apricot preserves or apricot spreadable fruit
- 2 teaspoons instant coffee crystals
- 1 egg yolk
- 1 teaspoon vanilla
- 1½ cups EQUAL® SPOONFUL*
- 3 egg whites
- ⅛ teaspoon cream of tartar
- ¼ cup all-purpose flour
- ⅛ teaspoon salt

Rich Chocolate Glaze
- 1 ounce semi-sweet chocolate
- 1 tablespoon stick butter or margarine
- Whipped topping, fresh raspberries and/or fresh mint (optional)

May substitute 36 packets Equal® sweetener.

• For Torte, heat 6 tablespoons butter, 4 ounces chocolate, milk, preserves and coffee crystals in small saucepan, whisking frequently until chocolate is almost melted.

• Remove pan from heat; continue whisking until chocolate is melted and mixture is smooth. Whisk in egg yolk and vanilla; add Equal®, whisking until smooth.

• Lightly grease bottom of 8-inch cake pan and line with parchment or waxed paper. Beat egg whites and cream of tartar to stiff peaks in large bowl. Fold chocolate mixture into egg whites; fold in combined flour and salt. Pour cake batter into pan.

• Bake in preheated 350°F oven 20 to 25 minutes or until wooden pick inserted in center comes out clean. Do not overbake. Carefully loosen side of cake from pan with small sharp knife, which will keep cake from cracking as it cools. Cool cake completely in pan on wire rack; refrigerate 1 to 2 hours or until chilled.

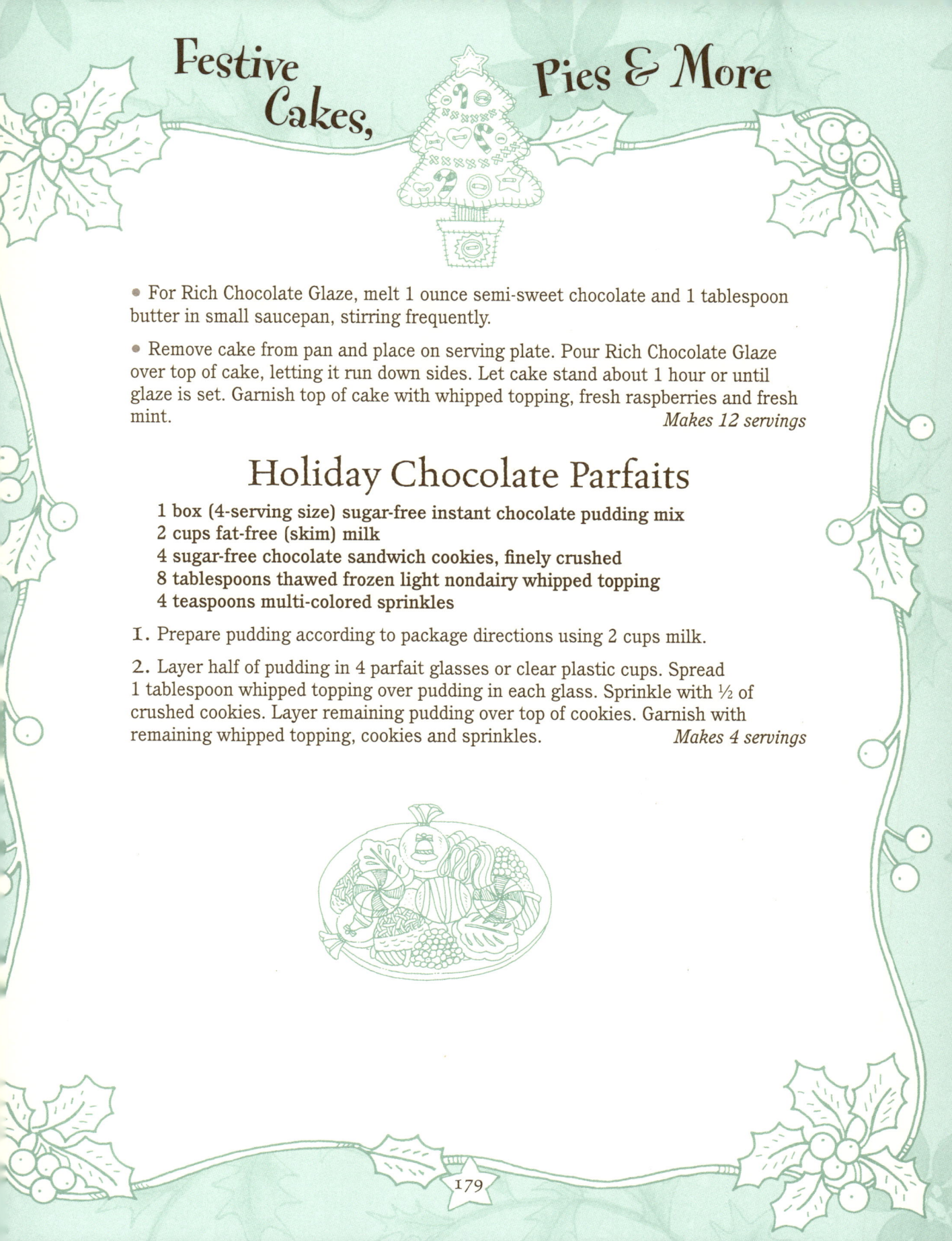

- For Rich Chocolate Glaze, melt 1 ounce semi-sweet chocolate and 1 tablespoon butter in small saucepan, stirring frequently.

- Remove cake from pan and place on serving plate. Pour Rich Chocolate Glaze over top of cake, letting it run down sides. Let cake stand about 1 hour or until glaze is set. Garnish top of cake with whipped topping, fresh raspberries and fresh mint.

Makes 12 servings

Holiday Chocolate Parfaits

1 box (4-serving size) sugar-free instant chocolate pudding mix
2 cups fat-free (skim) milk
4 sugar-free chocolate sandwich cookies, finely crushed
8 tablespoons thawed frozen light nondairy whipped topping
4 teaspoons multi-colored sprinkles

1. Prepare pudding according to package directions using 2 cups milk.

2. Layer half of pudding in 4 parfait glasses or clear plastic cups. Spread 1 tablespoon whipped topping over pudding in each glass. Sprinkle with ½ of crushed cookies. Layer remaining pudding over top of cookies. Garnish with remaining whipped topping, cookies and sprinkles.

Makes 4 servings

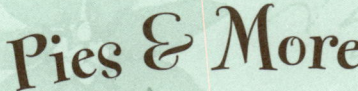
Christmas Cake with Creamy Eggnog Sauce

Cake
- 1 cup all-purpose flour
- ¾ cup butter or margarine, softened
- ½ cup DOMINO® Granulated Sugar
- 3 eggs
- 2 teaspoons vanilla
- 1 teaspoon imitation brandy extract and 2 teaspoons water *or* 1 tablespoon brandy *or* 1 tablespoon water
- 2 teaspoons cinnamon
- ½ teaspoon ground cloves
- ½ teaspoon nutmeg
- ¼ teaspoon salt
- ¼ teaspoon baking powder
- 1½ cups chopped pecans
- 1 cup raisins
- ¾ cup dried cranberries
- ½ cup dried currants

Creamy Eggnog Sauce
- ¾ cup DOMINO® Confectioners Sugar
- ¼ cup refrigerated or frozen nonfat egg product, thawed
- 3 tablespoons butter or margarine, melted
- ½ teaspoon vanilla
- ⅛ teaspoon nutmeg
- ½ cup whipping cream, softly whipped

Heat oven to 300°F. Generously grease and lightly flour 8×4-inch loaf pan. Combine all cake ingredients except nuts and fruits in large bowl; beat at low speed until moistened. Beat 2 minutes at medium speed. Stir in nuts and fruits. Spread batter evenly in pan. Bake 1 hour and 15 minutes to 2 hours or until toothpick inserted in center comes out clean. Cool 15 minutes. Remove from pan. Cool completely or serve warm.

For Creamy Eggnog Sauce, beat confectioners sugar, egg product, butter, vanilla and nutmeg in medium bowl until smooth. Fold in whipped cream. Serve with Christmas Cake.

Makes 16 servings

Tip: Cake can be wrapped in plastic wrap or foil and stored up to 2 weeks in refrigerator. Creamy Eggnog Sauce should be tightly covered and stored in refrigerator up to 8 hours.

Prep Time: 30 minutes
Bake Time: 2 hours
Cool Time: 15 minutes

Deep-Dish Pumpkin Pie

1¾ cups all-purpose flour
⅓ cup granulated sugar
⅓ cup firmly packed light brown sugar
1 cup (2 sticks) cold butter or margarine, cut into small pieces
1 cup chopped nuts
1 (15-ounce) can pumpkin
1 (14-ounce) can EAGLE BRAND® Sweetened Condensed Milk
  (NOT evaporated milk)
2 eggs
1 teaspoon ground cinnamon
½ teaspoon ground allspice
½ teaspoon salt

1. Preheat oven to 350°F. In medium mixing bowl, combine flour and sugars; cut in butter until crumbly. Stir in nuts. Reserve 1 cup crumb mixture; press remaining mixture firmly on bottom and halfway up sides of ungreased 12×7-inch baking pan.

2. In large mixing bowl, combine remaining ingredients except reserved crumb mixture; mix well. Pour evenly into crust. Top with reserved crumb mixture. Bake 55 minutes or until golden. Cool. Serve with ice cream, if desired. Refrigerate leftovers.

Makes 8 to 10 servings

 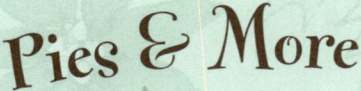
Cranberry Orange Cheesecake

1⅓ cups gingersnap crumbs
3 tablespoons EQUAL® SPOONFUL*
3 tablespoons stick butter or margarine, melted
3 packages (8 ounces each) reduced-fat cream cheese, softened
1 cup EQUAL® SPOONFUL**
2 eggs
2 egg whites
2 tablespoons cornstarch
¼ teaspoon salt
1 cup reduced-fat sour cream
2 teaspoons vanilla
1 cup chopped fresh or frozen cranberries
1½ teaspoons grated orange peel

*May substitute 4½ packets Equal® sweetener.

**May substitute 24 packets Equal® sweetener.

• Mix gingersnap crumbs, 3 tablespoons Equal® and melted butter in bottom of 9-inch springform pan. Reserve 2 tablespoons crumb mixture. Pat remaining mixture evenly onto bottom of pan. Bake in preheated 325°F oven 8 minutes. Cool on wire rack.

• Beat cream cheese and 1 cup Equal® in large bowl until fluffy; beat in eggs, egg whites, cornstarch and salt. Beat in sour cream and vanilla until blended. Gently stir in cranberries and orange peel. Pour batter into crust in pan. Sprinkle with reserved crumb mixture.

• Bake in 325°F oven 45 to 50 minutes or until center is almost set. Remove cheesecake to wire rack. Gently run metal spatula around rim of pan to loosen cake. Let cheesecake cool completely; cover and refrigerate several hours or overnight before serving. To serve, remove sides of springform pan.   *Makes 16 servings*

Traditional Fruit Cake

3 cups walnut halves
1 (4-ounce) package candied pineapple
1 (8-ounce) package candied cherries
1 (8-ounce) package chopped dates
¾ cup sifted all-purpose flour
¾ cup sugar
½ teaspoon baking powder
½ teaspoon salt
3 eggs, lightly beaten
3 tablespoons dark rum or rum extract
1 tablespoon grated orange peel
1 teaspoon vanilla

1. Preheat oven to 300°F. Line 9×5-inch loaf pan with greased waxed paper.

2. Combine nuts and fruit in large bowl; set aside.

3. Combine flour, sugar, baking powder and salt in medium bowl. Sift over nut mixture. Lightly toss dry ingredients and nut mixture together until nut mixture is well coated.

4. Blend in eggs, rum, orange peel and vanilla. Spread into prepared pan.

5. Bake 1 hour 45 minutes or until golden brown. Cool completely in pan on wire rack.

Makes 1 (9×5-inch) loaf

Pumpkin Cake with Orange Glaze

Cake
  2 cups boiling water
  ½ cup raisins
  2 cups granulated sugar
  1 cup melted Butter Flavor CRISCO® all-vegetable shortening
        or 1 Butter Flavor CRISCO® Stick plus more for greasing
  1 can (15 ounces) solid-pack pumpkin (not pumpkin pie filling)
  4 eggs
  2 cups all-purpose flour
  1 tablespoon ground cinnamon
  2 teaspoons baking powder
  1 teaspoon baking soda
  1 teaspoon ground ginger
  ¾ teaspoon salt
  ¼ teaspoon ground cloves

Orange Glaze
  1 cup confectioners' sugar
  1 tablespoon plus 1 teaspoon orange juice
  ¾ teaspoon grated orange peel
    Chopped walnuts

Vanilla Frosting Variation
  ¼ cup Butter Flavor CRISCO® all-vegetable shortening or ¼ Butter
        Flavor CRISCO® stick
  2 cups confectioners' sugar, sifted
  3 tablespoons milk
  1 teaspoon vanilla extract
    Chopped walnuts

I. Heat oven to 350°F. Grease 10-inch (12-cup) Bundt pan with Butter Flavor
CRISCO® Shortening. Flour lightly.

Cake

2. Pour boiling water over raisins in colander. Drain. Press lightly to remove excess water.

3. Combine granulated sugar, melted CRISCO® Shortening, pumpkin and eggs in large bowl. Beat at medium-high speed of electric mixer 5 minutes.

4. Combine flour, cinnamon, baking powder, baking soda, ginger, salt and cloves in medium bowl. Add to pumpkin mixture, 1 cup at a time, beating at low speed after each addition until blended. Stir in raisins with spoon. Pour into pan.

5. Bake at 350°F for 40 to 50 minutes or until toothpick inserted near center comes out clean. Cool 15 to 20 minutes before removing from pan. Place cake, top side up, on wire rack. Cool completely. Place cake on serving plate. Glaze or frost cake as desired.

Glaze

6. Combine confectioners' sugar, orange juice and orange peel in small bowl. Stir with spoon to blend. Spoon over top of cake, letting excess glaze run down side. Sprinkle with chopped nuts before glaze hardens.

Vanilla Frosting

7. Melt Butter Flavor CRISCO® in small saucepan on low heat. Transfer to medium bowl. Add confectioners' sugar. Beat at low, then high speed until blended.

8. Add milk and vanilla. Beat at high speed until smooth and frosting is of desired spreading consistency.

9. Spread frosting over top and side of cake. Sprinkle walnuts over top of cake.

Makes 1 (10-inch) bundt cake (12 to 16 servings)

Acknowledgments

The publisher would like to thank the companies and organizations listed below for the use of their recipes and photographs in this publication.

Birds Eye®
Blue Diamond Growers®
Bob Evans®
Cherry Marketing Institute
ConAgra Foods®
Dole Food Company, Inc.
Domino® Foods, Inc.
Eagle Brand®
Equal® sweetener
Filippo Berio® Olive Oil
Fleischmann's® Margarines and Spreads
Florida Department of Agriculture and Consumer Services, Bureau of Seafood and Aquaculture
Grandma's® is a registered trademark of Mott's, Inc.
Hershey Foods Corporation
Holland House® is a registered trademark of Mott's, Inc.
Lawry's® Foods
© Mars, Incorporated 2004
Mott's® is a registered trademark of Mott's, Inc.
National Pork Board
Nestlé USA
Norseland, Inc.
Lucini Italia Co.
Perdue Farms Incorporated
Reckitt Benckiser Inc.
Riviana Foods Inc.
Sargento® Foods Inc.
The J.M. Smucker Company
Sokol and Company
Splenda® is a registered trademark of McNeil Nutritionals
The Sugar Association, Inc.
Reprinted with permission of Sunkist Growers, Inc.
Uncle Ben's Inc.
Unilever Bestfoods North America
USA Rice
Walnut Marketing Board

Index

Index

Index

Index